HALLOWEEN

Halloween Magick . . .

Along with Halloween myths and lore, treats and goodies, divination techniques, harvest rituals and customs, you'll find spells, potions, and other Halloween magick for love, prosperity, and protection.

Porch Protection Turnips

If you have a front porch, these lanterns will shine protective light on your home Halloween Eve or Trick-or-Treating Night.

13 large turnips
    A sharp paring knife
13 tealight candles
    A hand drill
    Picture-hanging wire
    A black felt-tipped pen

Cut off the tops of the turnips. Discard tops. Hollow out enough of the turnip to drop in the tealight candle and protect the flame from the wind. With the hand drill, drill a hole on each side of the turnip an inch or so from the top (so you're cutting into the hollowed-out section), so the wire can loop through the hole. Secure, then loop through the opposite hole. Secure and cut wire. This will serve as the handle or hanger for your turnip. You can make the wire as long as you desire. Decorate the white area of the turnip with magickal symbols of protection, such as the rune Algiz (ᛉ). Hold your hands over the finished project, and say:

From dusk till dawn

Ancient protection I call hither

Blessings of those beyond the veil.

Hold your hands over the turnips until your palms grow warm or tingle and you feel good inside. When you are ready to use the turnips, light the candles, saying:

Blessings of Vesta upon this house.

Hang outside (or inside). Do not leave unattended. Bury on your property seven days after Samhain to continue the magickal protection of your property.

About the Author

"The best way for a magickal person to be accepted is to let people get to know you," explains Silver. "Once they understand your personal values and principles, their attitudes about your alternative religion interests tend to be more positive. Let them know you for the work that you do." Silver RavenWolf is a true Virgo who adores making lists and arranging things in order. The mother of four children, she will celebrate her nineteenth wedding anniversary in 1999. Silver extensively tours the United States, giving seminars and lectures about magickal religions and practices. It is estimated that Silver has met over 11,000 magickal individuals in the last three years.

To Write to the Author

If you wish to contact the author or would like more information about this book, please write to the author in care of Llewellyn Worldwide and we will forward your request. Both the author and publisher appreciate hearing from you and learning of your enjoyment of this book and how it has helped you. Llewellyn Worldwide cannot guarantee that every letter written to the author can be answered, but all will be forwarded. Please write to:

Silver RavenWolf
℅ Llewellyn Worldwide
P.O. Box 64383, Dept. K719-6
St. Paul, MN 55164-0383, U.S.A.

Please enclose a self-addressed, stamped envelope for reply, or $1.00 to cover costs.
Silver cannot get back to you unless you include a SASE!
If outside U.S.A., enclose international postal reply coupon.

Many of Llewellyn's authors have websites with additional information and resources. For more information, please visit our website at www.llewellyn.com.

SPELLS

HALLOWEEN

CUSTOMS

RECIPES

SILVER RAVENWOLF

2003 · Llewellyn Publications · St. Paul, Minnesota · 55164-0383 · U.S.A.

FIRST EDITION
Sixth Printing, 2003

Book design and editing by Rebecca Zins
Cover and interior art by Kathleen Edwards
Cover design and corn dolly illustrations by Anne Marie Garrison

Library of Congress Cataloging-in-Publication Data
RavenWolf, Silver, 1956–
    Halloween: customs, recipes & spells / Silver RavenWolf. —1st ed.
            p.   cm.
    Includes bibliographical references and index.
    ISBN 1-56718-719-6
    1. Halloween—History.   2. Magic.   3. Divination.   4. Witchcraft.
  I. Title.
  GT4965.R35   1999
  394.2646—dc21   99-29146
                                          CIP

Llewellyn Publications
A Division of Llewellyn Worldwide, Inc.
P.O. Box 64383, Dept. K719-6
St. Paul, MN 55164-0383, U.S.A.
www.llewellyn.com

Printed in the United States of America on recycled paper

Other Books
by Silver RavenWolf

To Stir a Magick Cauldron
To Ride a Silver Broomstick
To Light a Sacred Flame
American Folk Magick: Charms, Spells & Herbals
Angels: Companions in Magick
Witches Runes (formerly *The Rune Oracle*) (with Nigel Jackson)
Teen Witch
Teen Witch Kit
Silver's Spells for Prosperity
Silver's Spells for Protection
Silver's Spells for Love
Silver's Spells for Protection
Solitary Witch

Fiction

Beneath a Mountain Moon
Murder at Witches' Bluff
Witches' Night Out
Witches' Night of Fear
Witches' Key to Terror

Contents

The
Witches' Rune

Darksome night and shining moon
Hearken to the Witches' Rune.
East and South, West and North
Hear me now, I call thee forth.

By all the powers of land and sea
Be obedient unto me.
Wand and pentacle, cup and sword
Hearken ye unto my word.

Cord and censor, totem and knife
Waken ye all into life.
By all the powers of the Witches' blade
Come ye now as the charge is made.

Queen of Heaven, Queen of Hell
Send your aid unto my spell.
Horned Hunter of the Night
Work my will by magick rite.

By all the powers of Land and Sea
As I will, so mote it be.
By all the might of moon and sun
As I say, it shall be done.

—DOREEN VALIENTE[1]

1. English Craft author of many fine books on the subject, including *The Rebirth of Witchcraft; Witchcraft for Tomorrow;* and *An ABC of Witchcraft* (all published through Phoenix Publications, Custer, Washington). Although this poem appears all over the Internet with "author unknown," you will find the original version in *The Witches Bible* by Janet and Stewart Farrar (published through Magickal Childe). Doreen's books are required reading for my students of Craft history and practice.

Grab your flowing capes and come with me as we journey through the history and magickal practices of America's favorite scary holiday—Halloween! From Old World roots to New World charm, you'll learn about the hodgepodge of legends and customs that created our modern American Halloween holiday. From serious facts to fun, gossipy tidbits, we broom through time and space to bring you accurate, researched information, as well as practical, how-to goodies.

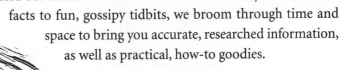

This comprehensive book contains historical information, modern magickal applications, yummy treats for your next Halloween party, tips on how to speak to the dead, and plenty of information about America's creepiest holiday.

So ghosts and goblins beware as we unveil . . .

the  truth about

Halloween!

INTRODUCTION

In early 1997, the owner of Llewellyn Worldwide decided to produce a book entitled "The Truth About Halloween" to assuage the many historical misconceptions held by the general public about this delightful holiday. He decided that the book should come from the pen of a magickal person, and asked me if I would like the project. My answer was a resounding "Yes!"

Every year when Halloween rolls around, the magickal community is inundated with requests for interviews that range from the truly serious and informative to the bizarre grocery-store-type hype. I receive many of these requests and was eager to delve further into a topic that often led the media to my door. Witches are not the only individuals called on during the month of October for that newshound hunting frenzy. You'll see interviews of pseudo-vampires, ghost hunters, psychics, and fiction writers that deal with occult subjects, as well as a nonstop plethora of horror films, both new and old, to enhance your viewing pleasure.

Almost every newspaper in the nation uses Halloween and harvest themes for ads and entertainment purposes. I could go on, but you get my drift.

More so than the other holidays the public currently enjoys, the American Halloween is often used as a political and religious kickball as real Witches (along with the rest of the folks mentioned) step into the limelight and grant newspaper interviews, visit radio talk shows, and greet television audiences across the country. It isn't that Witches push Halloween, it is that this is basically the only time the media is interested in the Witches, ghosts, goblins, and things that go bump in the night. In all honesty, it is rare for the media to look at the religion of Wicca at other times of the year, unless a discrimination case is so blatant (i.e., Congressman Barr against Wiccans in the military at Fort Hood in the spring and summer of 1999) that the community must step forward in a concerted effort to correct misinformation that is hundreds of years in error.

When I took on this project I thought it would be a snap. Do a little research, plug in some fun stuff, and presto-change-o (or should I say, "hocus-pocus"?) we've got a nifty little book on the history of Halloween combined with cool things to do during the month of October, and a great little tome for magickal people to wave and say, "here, this is the real history that may help you with your story." On to the next project. Done deal. Wrong. At the onset I discovered a horrible fact—although there are hundreds of books on the market today that carry a Halloween theme, less than a handful deal with accurately researched history of the holiday, from its Pagan roots to the present-day American institution of Halloween. When you limit an author's pool of research material, said author panics.

As I delved deeper into the history of Halloween, I knew I had a very real problem. History isn't always pretty. There are a lot of bad things lurking there. If I was going to honestly present my research, someone's nose was going to get out of joint simply because I am a magickal person, and therefore might hit too hard on current religious institutions. No one likes to think that there were bad people who did mean and nasty things in the name of one's religion, and if you list a particular religion by name people tend to ball up the doctrine and the history into one muddy snowball and be offended. As you read the first few chapters of this book, please don't practice guilt by association if you are not involved with a magickal religion. The historical information given is to render a mighty "thwap" to misinformation, not denigrate anyone's current religious choice. My editor, Becky Zins, was very helpful in making sure that the information is presented as realistically and honestly as possible.

chapter 1

THE SEARCH FOR HALLOWEEN

Druids would not know this night
And Witches would in wonder gaze
To see the festive costumed souls
That dash about the night in play
Where ancient magick ruled the land
Children's laughter fills the soul
Yet in this way the night is honored
Much like the ancients long ago.

—©1999 DAVID O. NORRIS

Witches' hats and harvest moon
Ghosts that dance to haunted tune.
Apples, goodies, food galore
Halloween has this and more.

Fairies, gnomes, and funny clowns
Mom and I go 'round the town.
Cats and pumpkins, friends to meet
Everyone says "trick or treat"!

Harvest moon, velvet sky, pumpkins glowing, children laughing, costumes, candy, snapping breezes . . . scary stories, Indian corn, haunted houses, smiling scarecrows, blowing leaves . . . apples, parties, spindly spiders, dancing bats, grinning ghosts, sparkling stars . . . hayrides, dances, screeching cats, big bonfires . . . just where did this autumn gaiety begin? Let's look through those cobwebby corridors of time to unearth the exciting genealogy of the American celebration we call Halloween!

The Wild Hunt

Nothing is ever as simple as it seems—especially when dealing with history. Too often events and circumstances of our past were written or rewritten by people who, for whatever reason, operated under an agenda or simply wanted history to reflect how it should have been, rather than how it was. We also have the tainted research—unsubstantiated information written by one person, used by another person as a reputable source, and so on, which keeps gathering like a dirty snowball, leaving you with watery myth and muddy facts. How, then, do we determine what is fact and what is fiction? In some cases, we can't. In other situations, we dig.

Halloween, like any other subject, has a lengthy lineage. If we dig deeply enough, we discover that Halloween has a three-pronged history, like a pitchfork; therefore, we have three avenues of research: Pagan Practices; Christian Practices; and American Practices. Like the pitchfork (which is often used in harvest or Halloween celebrations for decoration), the three prongs of history meet together at the handle, creating our modern-day assumption of Halloween. To really knock your socks off, I'll tell you that our American Halloween and the holiday of Thanksgiving have much the same history.

(Excuse me just a moment. I have to warm up our transportation. Brooms can be so fussy if you expect them to take off cold.)

Paleopagan[1] Practices

All Hallows Eve, Halloween, Samhain, All Hallows, Spirit Night, Hallow E'en, Saven—our journey into history takes us back long before the rise of the Roman Empire or the birth of Christ, long before anyone decided it might be a good idea to write things down in a manner where the information could be saved for future generations. Yes, there was a semblance of oral history, but 4,000 years before Christ and the 2,000 years hence (give or take a few years) is a long time to keep anything intact, especially if it has been through word of mouth. Current historical guestimates on the age of this holiday hover around 4000 B.C.E. Just think about that for a moment. If you celebrate Halloween today, you are taking part in a holiday festivity that has a genealogical line of more than 6,000 years. For something to have survived that long—through the tides of human passion, war, famine, and religious persecution—surely is a magnificent feat!

Our first stop on the Halloween Trail puts us at the historical favorite of 4000 B.C.E. Here we are, standing among tribal peoples who have split their year in half the only way they know how. In the spring (close to our modern May Day), the people send their domesticated animals out of safe enclosures to graze on the open land. The sun has warmed the earth and given birth to vegetation on which the animals survive. This is the celebration of Beltainne (or Beltane), and is considered the light half of the year. The second portion of the year (around our modern Halloween), the people bring the animals back to a safe haven because they know that the earth is preparing for her long sleep.

As we stand together on a hilltop, we are ringed by bonfires and dancing, happy people. Can you hear the beat of the stamping feet? Can you smell the autumn scent in the tendrils of smoke? Can you feel the change of the earth's seasons deep within your soul? Gaze into the flames of the fire and connect with the ancient, primal force of the Paleopagan. Reach out to the flames of transformation.

Fire, to these people, was a physical symbol of divinity. Perhaps they kindled fires on earth to match the fire of the sun or the lights of the stars. Throughout history, fire equates to the element of clearing, a vehicle of eradication, so it is not unusual that

fire would work itself into many religious celebrations. Fire also keeps us warm and allows us to see things at night (no electric lights here). Among ancient peoples, no matter the territory or the culture, fire often represented an aspect of the divine. Stand here for a moment, and enjoy the Spirit of the divine as you connect with the ancient history of Halloween. We can't tarry long, though. We've got lots to see, for at some point in time, these people will become known as the Celts, and they have a compendium of history that entwines with our modern Halloween!

The Celts

Before we land, we need to circle while your flight attendant (that's me) gives you some historical information on the Celts so that you will be comfortable upon disembarking from the broom. Please remember that seat backs and tray tables must be in an upright position as we make our descent.

Many historians feel that the greatest strength of the Celtic peoples involves their collective mythos, but wading through the romanticism to find unmodified information can prove a tricky endeavor. If you want to start a fistfight among scholars, begin touting your opinions on the historical accuracies (or inaccuracies) of the Celtic peoples in today's literature. You could leave the room and the fracas would continue, therefore I tread lightly and give you enough information to pique your interest. You will find a healthy bibliography at the back of this book should you choose to dive into the information muck of the early Celts. Some authors call Celtic history the shapeshifting of knowledge.[2]

According to *The Book of Druidry* by Ross Nichols (see bibliography), the Celts are now believed to be a really very ancient race, the first of the large-scale migrants who dispersed in separate waves into Europe about 2300 B.C.E., followed by another wave a bit later. The landing and subsequent dispersal from eastern Mediterranean voyages appears to be Spain, and the cultures most likely moved from there to Ireland and western Britain. Let us not discount the movement south to Anatolia and Palestine. Regardless of who moved where and when they did it, one fact is certain: they moved, although this movement took centuries and was quite costly in terms of the blood bank of the universe. According to Isaac Bonewits, current archeological theory is that as much of the transmission of Indo-European languages and their once-associated gene pools may have occurred through the peaceful transfer of knowledge (and exchange of spouses) between neighboring tribes as through warfare.[3]

Moving our flaps at the appropriate degrees as we land, we find ourselves in pre-Christian Europe, approximately 350 B.C.E., where the Celtic invasion introduced a new cultural strain to Ireland and Britain. The Celts are listed as a subfamily of the Indo-European family. The people are pastoral, meaning that they raise animals. They've got themselves a religion and the festival they are celebrating is a harvest one, which lasts approximately three days. The Indo-European cultures appear to have a caste system that affects social, political, magickal, and religious functions. From the royalty to the outsiders, everyone seems to have had some sort of nomenclature. We find musicians, historians, astronomers, genealogists, judges, diviners, poets, and, of course, religious personages.[4]

For those of you who are into astrology, we are exactly at fifteen degrees Scorpio. The Celtic peoples celebrated four festivals, called fire festivals, commonly known today as Samhain, Candlemas, Beltainne, and Lughnasadh. Four additional days of Germanic origin—the solstices and the equinoxes—also crept into the Indo-European cultures, though where and when is debatable, and as we are concerned primarily with Halloween, we'll just leave it at that.

The festival we are visiting has a name: Samhain. Though if we were in the Scottish Highlands, the name would be 'sav-en,' or in Wales, 'sow-een.' This is the summer's end festival and, more importantly, it is the Celtic New Year. The two themes are celebrating the dead and divining for the future, so no matter where we walk, there is revelry and seriousness (kinda like this book). The celebration commences at sundown, so let's get ready to party! I personally am hoping they have drums, because my little feet like to dance to that primordial beat.

What does the word "Samhain" mean? Step aside here. Yes, let's gather in our own little tour group . . . careful, don't trip over that guy, he's doing a divination. Well, we know what the word Samhain *doesn't* mean. There is no archeological or literary evidence of a Celtic (or Druid) god by the name of Samhain. This little slip of fact appears to have begun in the 1700s by two authors: Higgins (published in 1827), where he quotes Col. Charles Vallency, and someone by the name of Pictet who tried very hard to associate Samhain with a biblical reference to a sun deity. Bostwick (originally published in 1894) associates "Samhuin" (sic) with the moon, but translates "Samhain" correctly, though he tries to derive the roots of Gaelic and Erse from Latin.[5] Indeed, the name of the British Celtic god of the dead was Gwynn ap Nudd (for the Welsh, Arawn). The Irish didn't have a "lord of death" in their belief system. The Scottish-Gaelis Dictionary will tell you that Samhain means "Summer's End." "Sam" plus "Fuin" equals "Samhain"—or Hallowtide, Feast of All Souls.[6]

Legends indicate that on Samhain, all the hearth fires in Ireland were doused and then lit again from a central fire maintained by the Druids at Tlachtga, twelve miles from the royal hill of Tara. A central fire of this nature is called a need-fire. The Celts believed Samhain and Beltainne represented mystical fissures in time that allowed the living access to the land of the dead, called Tir na n'Og. To the Celtic peoples, there was death in life, and life in death—a concept no religion has shaken in the past 3,000 years. We must remember that the ancient view of time was cyclical, not linear, and in this framework New Year's Eve as Samhain represents a point outside of time, when the natural order of the universe dissolves back into primordial chaos, preparatory to reestablishing itself in a new order. Thus, Samhain is a night that exists outside of time, and hence it may be used to view any other point in time.[7]

As the Celtic religious system grew, so did their beliefs involving human afterlife and the care of the dead, as all religious beliefs (before and after the Celts) have implemented. Some historians speculate that it was the Christians who brought forth the idea of actually burying the dead in the ground, caves, or manmade catacombs. This idea sprang from their belief that on the final day of reckoning on earth, the faithful would be taken into heaven—a concept absolutely foreign to the early Celts. The Celtic practice of disposing human remains involved the funeral pyre and the sacred fire. This spiritual practice was also practical. Disposing of the remains by fire helped keep the spread of disease in check and discouraged grave robbing.

As I mentioned earlier, to the Celts, what you would commonly call "heaven" today was a place called Tir na n'Og; however, please keep in mind that the Celts had no concept of heaven or hell. It is especially important that we realize the ancient Celts did not fear their dead. The custom of leaving food at the table (the birth of the "treat" part of trick-or-treat) was a gesture of welcoming to those departed. From these visits came the idea that those who had gone beyond the land of the living could provide information on past or future events, thus the practice of divination in conjunction with Samhain was born. It was also believed that the dead could assist the living in practical and spiritual matters. If the dead did a good deed for you, he or she would be rewarded and assisted in the elevation process of the afterlife; therefore, ancestor veneration was a normal part of Celtic life because they believed that if the dead helped you, they could earn brownie points on their side of the veil. We know that the Celts sincerely believed in an afterlife because they would promise to pay debts "in the next life."

The modern concepts of demons and devils was not a part of the Celtic religious system. The Celts did believe, however, in the faery folk, whom they thought may inhabit the land of the dead (the land of in-between), and peek out now and then to associate with humans on an incredibly limited basis. Elves weren't regarded as evil but, as W. J. Bethancourt says, "very different and very dangerous to mess with."[8]

The faeries, who lived in numerous mounds or sidhe (pronounced "shee," also used as a title for faery), were thought to be resentful of humankind for overtaking their land and forcing them to inhabit the in-between. Some of these faeries were considered hostile and, because time and space could be conquered on Samhain, faeries were said to roam the countryside, creating mischief and, now and then, kidnapping a human or two (just for fun, you understand)—except the humans never came back. Ooops. Here, then, is the root of the scary stuff associated with Halloween. The mischief, of course, was caused by living and breathing humans, and accepted by the Celts as a psychological release before the onset of winter gloom and doom (though I doubt they would have explained it in those terms). Practical jokes were accepted, especially when you were walking in the woods in the middle of the night.[9]

Is it odd, gross, or unusual that a group of people should set aside a day for the dead? No. Different cultures and religions have followed such a practice for centuries.

The Festival of Souls, called Obon or Bon, is celebrated in Japan on July 13 (lunar calendar) or August 15 (solar calendar). In Mexico we have El Dia de los Muertos, or the Day of the Dead, celebrated between October 27 and November 2. The Chinese celebrate Ching Ming or Tomb Sweeping Day, which falls between April 5 or 6, depending on their calendar, and has been popular in China since 3700 B.C.E. In the Philippines we've got an All Saints' Day fiesta, and in Germany we have Walpurgis (Walpurgisnacht) falling on April 30, just to name a few. If you will look to your left, you will see a priestess of the Clan holding a rite for the dead, and I'm told that our schedule includes a ceremony for a prosperous new year.

All passengers, please prepare to board Silver Flight 2000. Our in-flight movie will contain information about the Druids, a religious subset of the Paleopagan peoples. Please refrain from using cellular phones or other electronic devices during takeoff.

The Druids

If you ask any individual today who is practicing Druidism just what, exactly, a Druid is, they will probably tell you first and foremost that Druidism is a way of life that uses the foundation of respect, dignity, development of study and virtue, and the belief in the supreme power of the universe, give or take a few ideologies. Trying to define the ancient Druidic religion and caste system is another cauldron of debate, and since we don't want any turbulence on this flight, we'll try to stick to the bare minimum of facts, with enough information to refute some of the odd accusations you may have heard about the ancient Druids in relation to the Samhain/Halloween festivities of the Paleopagans.[10]

Keep in mind that there were many Celtic tribes and only the western Celtic clergy (the Druids) are the subject of this in-flight dissertation, and that, currently, the reign of the Druid priesthood is calculated to be approximately 500 years—meaning that not all Paleopagans were Druids and not all Samhain Paleopagan celebrations involved Druidry. There is so little information available on this era in history that we must be hesitant in drawing any conclusions on the Druid caste system. There were full and part-time healers, those who worked with the weather, the stars, the laws of the land, those who were able to move with political finesse, midwives, supervisors of public ritual, historians . . . we could go on, but you get the picture. It is also debatable whether or not these individuals functioned as clergy full-time, or only part-time. Some historians believe that the individual Druid lived alone and shared in the lives of the people. Others feel that they were constantly a part of the people. Regardless, the Druid caste is seen as individuals (both male and female) well versed in all learning and considered to have the gift of prophecy. They could impose the geis, a kind of taboo that was both an injunction and a prohibition. If you ignored the injunction, you could incur dishonor or death. Kings and chiefs alike had to await the words of the Druid before making major decisions for the people.

Unfortunately, as is obvious of early humanity, the Druids didn't write anything down. They functioned as judges, ambassadors, and religious leaders, and there appears to be more than one wave of Druidic faith[11] that included an older sect who worked with wood circles, then stone, and who were not too delighted to share all their innermost secrets with the constant Celtic invasion. Just like in America, with our various experiences with the migration of peoples, so too do we find such a phenomena in Celtic history. This could account for the confusion in what the Celts may have looked like, as descriptions range from small and dark-haired to tall, fair-skinned, and fair-haired.[12] The advent of possible Roman rule and subsequent beliefs in Christianity heralded the downfall of the Druidic caste, though some historians believe that in Ireland the Druidic caste infiltrated all other castes, including the early aspects of the Celtic Christian Church. It is from the Druidic caste that many current magickal religions trace a portion of their roots, including the modern Druid and many Wiccan sects. We know that the Roman Julius Caesar found the Druids of Gaul to be a main obstacle, as the Druids urged the resistance of Roman takeover, thus sealing the fate of the Druids and their religious system.[13]

It is generally agreed upon by current scholars that the Druids did not build Stonehenge and that at least fifty percent of the Druid caste may have included women and children. Throughout the ancient Celtic world, before Christianity or political conquest entered into the reckoning, there were Druidic assemblies and possibly larger teaching units or colleges.[14] We have to be careful when reading the accounts by Caesar of Rome because he was basically trying to convince everyone that the Celts and Germanic peoples were barbarians and therefore should be conquered for the good of their own self-interest. His pontificating on the Druids is subject to extreme scrutiny—yet, in his own way, good old Julius helped to keep the memory of the Druids and their celebration of Samhain alive and well into the twenty-first century.

We are cruising at 32,000 feet and, if you would look to your left, we are going to do a quick fly-by of ancient Rome. Yes, beautiful view, isn't it? Please keep your seat belts fastened, as the history here is filled with turbulence, and until we reach America I prefer to stay in the air until it's safe to land.

A Fly-By of Ancient Rome

Why on earth should we care about ancient Rome when we're talking about Halloween? Let us return to the in-flight movie to discover the significance of the Roman regime. Let me begin by saying that Rome had the habit of changing rulers as many times as you empty the lint trap in your dryer. Between 14 and 37 C.E., Christianity began its rise in Rome but would not take total control for another three hundred years. By 41 C.E., Claudius distinguished himself to the Roman senate by accomplishing the conquest of Britain. The Romans also had a harvest festival called the Festival of Pomona, celebrated on November 1, which they introduced to the Celtic peoples. Pomona was the goddess of the orchards and the harvest. As the Festival of Pomona covered the same general period as Samhain, the Celts didn't have much trouble blending the two holidays together. By the first century C.E., Romans and Celts inhabited the same scattered villages throughout much of the old Celtic world, allowing for the survival of the ancient harvest festival known as Samhain. The Romans never conquered or even invaded Ireland, therefore, historically, we don't have a Roman overlay on Irish folklore and myth before the advent of Christianity. When viewing Halloween history through Scottish eyes, we need to remember that although Scotland was invaded, it was never conquered by Rome. The people we know as Scots are actually an amalgamation of Norse, Pict, and Irish that happened well after the Romans left Britain.[15]

Around two hundred years later (314 C.E.), Constantine the Great declared the Roman Empire a Christian one, closing a door on the Celtic religion. The fate of Samhain and the Druids was sealed. In other areas of Europe, the Celtic religious structure deteriorated as the Romans systematically murdered the Druid priests

and priestesses, seeing them as stumbling blocks to the Roman order of things. The Druids became the hunted and, when caught, they faced certain death.

The Growth of Christianity

By the fourth and fifth centuries C.E., Celtic Christianity slithered into Ireland. St. Patrick had his hands full and here's where the kettle starts to boil. At first, the Pagan peoples openly welcomed Christianity (as they openly welcomed the beliefs of other people), but as Christianity filtered into the Celtic system, the church officials had a few problems—mainly, the Celts didn't want to give up their holidays or many of their folk practices. They were unwilling to throw out traditions ingrained in their family and social structure for hundreds of years. If you can't get someone to completely change, what do you do? I believe the operative word here is "bribe." And that's exactly what happened. The Germanic Yule changed to Christmas (December 25 is actually the birthday of Pagan god Mithra, a solar deity); the Celtic Oimelc to Easter; and Samhain to All Hallows Eve.

To make the Pagan peoples adhere more closely to this new religion of Christianity, the clergy of the day taught the peasants that the faeries were really demons and devils (remember, a concept totally unknown to Celtic belief or history) and that their beloved dead were horrid ghosts and ghouls. The early Christians erroneously associated the Celtic land of the dead with the Christian concept of hell—enter the making of evil that had no basis in fact and was absolutely rooted in fear. And, if that wasn't acceptable, these early Christians made up new myths; for example, that the faeries were really angels who had neither sided with God nor the Devil, and were therefore condemned to walk the earth and scare the bejesus out of everyone until Judgment Day. Pope Gregory I declared:

> Let the shrines of idols by no means be destroyed. Let water be consecrated and sprinkled in the temples, let altars be erected . . . so that the people, not seeing their temples destroyed, may displace error and recognize and adore the true God . . . And because they were wont to sacrifice to devils, some celebration should be given in exchange for this . . . they should celebrate a religious feast and worship God by their feasting, so that still keeping outward pleasure, they may more readily receive spiritual joys.[16]

To help the belief in Christianity along, the Druids were systematically murdered. The early Christians also taught the area peasants that their Lord of the Underworld was, in fact, Satan—which is ridiculous, as the two mythos don't have anything in common. It appears that the Christians misunderstood what the word "Samhain" meant and, because the peasants used this celebration to honor the dead, assumed that Samhain was the incorrect pronunciation of a Pagan deity in the Bible, recorded as Samuel, from the Semitic *Sammael*, meaning the God of the Underworld. Sammael, while we're at it, is also the name of an angel who also appears to have a checkered past, depending on which religious scholar you're talking to. The early Christians then made up a deity that wasn't, and still isn't, real.

Keep in mind that one's religious persuasion has nothing to do with one's genetic structure, therefore let us not assume that the peasants were stupid and the Christians smart. They were all people—equal in mind, body, and spirit. The Celtic peoples reveled in superstition and the early Christian missionaries used these superstitions to their advantage. Where once Samhain centered on activities to honor the Gods for the harvest, prepare for the winter months by asking for protection, and welcome the spirits of their loved ones, now this turn of the year stank of decomposing corpses, demons salivating for souls, and hell fires waiting to consume unsuspecting little peasants. The early Catholic Church thought that if they made the holiday frightening, they could stop it. When this didn't work, they used the holiday to their advantage, teaching the peasants that if they did not pay their taxes and give hefty donations, the evil mythos that the church created would destroy the unfaithful. And when church and state demand that you believe something or die, you usually believe it.

I hope you are enjoying your flight on the Silver 2000, brought to you by the Witches of America. Please remember to stop at the desk when we reach America to credit your frequent flier miles. Now, on to the topic of the Witches, which is the next area of history that we will view safely from the air.

The Witches

So far, we've talked about the bonfires, the land of the dead, how the early Christians managed to superimpose Satan onto Samhain, and when faeries got zapped into demons with a bit of myth-remaking and holy water—but no mention of Witches, commonly associated in our time with Halloween. Where did the Witches come from? Did they just pop on the planet from another dimension? Did they arrive in a spaceship? Did the devil have a ritual and conjure them up to frighten innocent Christians?

Naw.

Women and men of magick, healing, and prophecy have appeared in every culture and in every social system in the world—and, of course, you had them in the Celtic territories of Britain, Scotland, Germany, France, Spain, and Ireland. WitchCraft was not, in itself, a religion, but more of a system of magick inherent in the Pagan religious mythos. It is thought that the Craft grew out of the dissemination of the Druid caste, which opened the magickal practices up to the common individual, thus dispersing the customs and the fabric of the magick among the many, and drawing in information from mystery traditions all over the world. WitchCraft today means "Craft of the Wise" and has grown into a religion of its own, primarily due to the misinformation spouted by the early Christian Church and the persecution campaign mounted by that church to eradicate the ancient Pagan religious structure, including the Celtic, Germanic, and Roman Pagan faiths. Some modern Witches believe that the word Witch means "to bend," and was applied to sorcery and healing even during the reign of the Druidic caste—being neither a negative or positive connotation. You will also hear that Witch comes from the Anglo-Saxon word "wicce," meaning "Wise One," and some conclude that the early Christians created the actual word "Witch" to stand for all that they didn't believe in, no matter what might fall under that heading at any particular time in history. We should also add that those who held onto their Pagan belief of male and female divinity became known as Witches. Although some of Margaret Murry's work on the history of the Craft[17] has been discounted (her investigation supporting a semiorganized Witch religion in Europe), we should not discount the grains of truth she may have unearthed. Is the Craft a result of Druidry, as some feel? Or was the Craft a line of family and Pagan practices that developed on its own? This question, as we near the turn of the century, has not been answered.

The "man is boss" concept did not begin with the early Christians, but with the Roman citizenry. Roman women were already laboring under a patriarchal thumb—even though the goddesses of that culture were revered, their human counterparts did not enjoy such freedom.[18]

This was particularly hard for the Celtic women to stomach, since the Celts believed in and practiced equality. When the early Christian clergy began shoveling the "I am male (pound chest), do as I say" stuff onto the peasants, the thought didn't go over well at all. When people won't listen to those in power, those in power tend to get nasty. We are now coming to the blood and guts portion of the Halloween story, where the early Christian clergy and their henchmen used mass murder and torture to drive their point home.

Who did they kill?

Why, the Witches, of course.

And who were the Witches?

The women.

The Burning Times

The seat of almost every religion known today, whether it is acknowledged or not, belongs to the women. It has always been so. No, I don't mean that ladies are better than gentlemen. Bear with me here, as we work through this together. By studying ancient religions all over the world, we discover that most of these structures honored both women and men, and allowed women to have high station within the hierarchy. Divinity, too, was seen as both male and female, with women encouraged do the work of the religion. Not so in Christianity, a thoroughly male-opinionated structure taken from the Roman practices of the day. Christ himself did not support male domination and spoke out against it—his followers, including Peter and Paul, had different thoughts on the matter, and began twisting Christ's teachings to fit their own view of how a religion should be, keeping in step with the Roman belief that the woman should remain secluded in the home. Sexuality, however, was a large part of early Roman belief—something that the early Christians would not tolerate. A Roman woman would be banished if she was unfaithful to her husband. A Roman man could be unfaithful to his wife, as long as he was with a registered prostitute. Therefore, patriarchal practices did not begin with the early Christians—the denigration of women began with the Roman Empire and was accepted by the early Christians. We should note also that it was the Roman Empire that produced the popular slave trade—conquering vast communities, killing the men, and taking the women and children. Although Christ did not believe in slaves, those Christians who followed him felt there was nothing wrong with the practice, and so the slave trade persisted. A Roman father could kill any of his children, and had complete rule over his home—another institution of thought that was carried over into the Christian religion. Many Christians of today have no idea how much of the New Testament was based not on Christ's ideas, but rather on Roman thought and rules instead.

Peter, Paul, and others like them took advantage of Christ's death and shaped the new religion to their own purposes, setting the stage for the heinous crimes perpetrated by church and state in the centuries to come. In our society, women keep the holy days, train the children, and provide the labor and the cohesive socialization of the church, yet they often go unacknowledged and without power in the governmental decisions of the religions they belong to. This is a direct result of the Roman structure and persecution of the early Christian Church.

Evil, as much as we'd like to lay the blame elsewhere, does not belong to some strange entity floating around, rubbing its clawed hands in delight, salivating about what it can force us to do. It is my firm belief that we humans create the evil in the world and are too chicken to take responsibility for what our minds, hearts, and hands have wrought in negative circumstances. Humans find great joy in laying the responsibility on some mythical being rather than owning up to what we have, in error, created ourselves. Rather than taking the blame for mass murder, the early Christian Church chose to blame the creation of evil on Satan, even as they burned and mutilated innocent people.

During the Dark Ages, the church sought to eradicate the Pagans and wise women from the countryside so that it could amass both power and property. First, they had to devalue women. The church taught, among other things, that women had no souls and therefore were not important. Once this had occurred, it was only a small step to make women inhuman. The church was able to incite the superstitious populace by making the situation an "us or them" proposition. Once you have made a group of people inhuman, then you remove the guilt of murder.

In essence, the church developed a marketing plan to sell Christianity and, much like the political marketing plans today, used various methods to push their product, including fear, torture, and misinformation. During this process the church incorporated many of the already firmly entrenched beliefs of the country folk, like the Yule log, Christmas trees, gargoyles to guard churches, the Easter bunny, and so on, into church custom and policy so as to keep the people they were trying to brainwash happy. The church even took the Pagan gods and goddesses and turned them into saints—St. Brigit, as a case in point. When the church could not convince the people to give up their Pagan ways, they moved to stronger methods. During the Dark Ages, historians believe that approximately 1.5 million women and children were murdered by the Witch Finders. This era is commonly called "The Burning Times."

In the eighth century, a document written by the church entitled the *Canon Episcopi* declared that the Witches were an illusion but, at the same time, the church also created a very deadly weapon—The Inquisition.[19] The leaders of the Inquisition overturned this document, and thus began their wicked persecution of innocent people all across Europe with the full sanction of the church.[20] Most persecutions took place between the fifteenth and seventeenth centuries. By the time these fanatics were through, the female population had dipped to an alarming rate and almost no wise women or local healers had survived. During that time, religious leaders changed the Bible, particularly in one passage where it still says, "Thou shalt not suffer a witch to live." In the original language of the Bible, the wording was, "Thou shalt not suffer a poisoner to live." (You can thank King James for that little misprint—but then, a king can do anything he wants, can't he?) As you can see, the men of the Inquisition ruled with an iron hand, even to the point of changing many of the passages in the Bible to suit their own purposes and free themselves from the responsibility of their own evil.

Perhaps the most significant turning point in the fate of the church and the impact upon Samhain and the Pagan religions occurred on November 11, 1215, when Pope Innocent III opened the Fourth Lateran Council where church officials gathered in Rome from the many surrounding kingdoms as well as far more distant states. Although many issues were discussed in a thirty-day period (later councils were to last years), the most significant points were the creation of papal courts for dispensing justice (removing the meddling of local lords and kings alike from church business and law) and the insistence that excommunication and the removal of nonbelievers was not enough—they had to be silenced. Permanently.[21] Executions, up until this point, were uncontrolled and often thwarted by means of money, political power, or family lineage.

During the eighteenth century, the horror that had sucked the life out Europe's population began to dwindle. Many historians call the beginning of this time the Age of Reason, meaning people actually began to think about what was happening around them rather than going along just to keep peace. In 1736, WitchCraft ceased to be an offense punishable by death in England and Scotland.[22] In 1722, the last documented Witch burning in the British Isles took place in Scotland, when a woman by the name of Janet Horne was executed. But a look at history, even into the early twentieth century, shows occasional burnings and hangings involving suspected Witches. In England, in 1952, the government repealed the last of the WitchCraft laws, meaning it was no longer a crime to practice the religion of WitchCraft in that country.

The end of WitchCraft as a crime in which one lost one's life to the bloody hands of the persecutors came at various times in different countries. The dates of the last executions are as follows: Holland—1610; England—1684; America—1692; Scotland—1727; France—1745; Germany—1775; Switzerland—1782; Poland—1793; Italy—1791 (although the last individual was given a reprieve). What made them stop? Self preservation of the living. Germany was forced to curtail the actions of religious fanatics because whole towns were accused. In the words of Rossell Hope Robbins, Fellow of the Royal Society of Literature, speaking of the travesty against innocent people, "Never were so many, so wrong, for so long."[23]

Today in the United States, Wicca or WitchCraft is considered a viable religion (not a cult) and U. S. Army personnel are permitted to claim Wicca as their choice of religion on their dog tags, although at the writing of this book, religious fanatics are trying to force the military to discriminate against the Wiccan religion.

So how did Witches become evil, and why did the Christians associate them primarily with Halloween?

The Celtic women were the stronghold of the family environment and, although the Celts accepted Christianity at first, they did not want to give up their family traditions or their lifestyle. Celts were free-thinking people. The church was not into free thinking, therefore anything that did not follow church dictates was evil, according to the church. Hence the Witches (really the women) became "evil." Since Samhain was the primary festival of the Celts (their New Year, and therefore important), and the church had already determined that Samhain was evil, the association between Witches and Halloween was born. On one level this link was correct—the Pagan peoples did celebrate Samhain; however, the manner in which the church presented the holiday (and some still insist today)—that Samhain and the Pagan peoples were evil—is, as we have seen from our fly-by, incorrect.

All Saints' Day, All Souls' Day, All Hallows Eve, Hallowmas

The original celebration of All Saints' Day is attributed to Pope Boniface IV, who dedicated the Roman temple, the Pantheon, consecrated as the Church of the Blessed Virgin and all Martyrs on May 13, 610 C.E.[24] This day was to honor those Christians who had been murdered for their beliefs without official recognition for their dedication to the faith.

All Saints' Day and All Hallows Eve (Halloween) were reintroduced by Pope Gregory III in the seventh century C.E. The date was changed to November 1 because those Annoying Pagans just refused to cough up their original Samhain. (Remember that October 31 was the eve of Samhain and November 1 the day of Samhain.) Harvest festivals, despite Christianity, continued in Europe. Pope Gregory IV gave the custom official authorization in 835 C.E. and extended the celebration to include all saints. The day was to honor God and the saints, known and unknown. Saints, of course, are exemplary individuals who have died for the cause of the church or who, in some way, have been of service to the people. Perhaps because of this day's association with the honoring of the dead and the difficulty experienced by church officials to eradicate the fire festival of Samhain, the celebration was moved to November 1 to supplant Pagan beliefs. All Saints' Day became Hallowmas—a mass to honor the dead. The Eve of All Hallows Day, October 31, became All Hallows Even, which evolved into the word Hallowe'en. Although the church wished this time to be one of somber prayer and quiet custom, the vigorous Celts continued their practices of bonfires and fortunetelling. In the church's favor, however, is their insistence that the peasants offer prayers instead of sacrifices.[25] As we've seen, though, the early church did quite a lot of sacrificing human flesh to the hangman's noose and burning pyres on their own, meaning it was okay to kill someone as long as the church sanctioned the killing. The church also convinced the people that the need-fires, kindled in honor of the cycle of the seasons, would instead keep away the devil.[26]

All Souls' Day is a bit different. This festival falls on November 2 and, in the Roman Catholic Church, was a day to offer prayers and alms to assist the souls of those departed who managed to get stuck in Purgatory—an in-between place that is neither heaven nor hell. It is thought that this celebration was first instituted in the monasteries of Cluny, France, in 988 C.E. by the Benedictine abbot Saint Odilo, though various scholars argue as to the original date (some saying 993 C.E.). All Souls' Day became a general celebration among the European peoples and an excuse to revive many of their pre-Christian folk customs. The feast day was approved by Pope Sylvester II around 1000 C.E.

On Halloween, October 31, 1517, Martin Luther initiated a religious reformation that put a halt to the observance of the holiday for many Europeans. Martin Luther of Germany, John Calvin of Geneva, and others developed a new concept that removed icons from Christianity and rejected the authority of the Pope. Old customs die hard, however, and the Protestant Christians held autumnal festivals entwined in their secular rights.

When a political plot masterminded by fanatical Catholic leaders and a Catholic revolutionary by the name of Guy Fawkes backfired (known as the "gunpowder plot"), Fawkes was executed. The Protestant Parliament passed an act in January 1606 declaring November 5 a day of national thanksgiving—celebration of the triumph of Protestants over Catholics. Many Protestant Christians then used the holiday as an excuse for celebrating the old autumnal customs.

Over the succeeding centuries Halloween, like Christmas, picked up various customs and discarded others, depending on the complex socialization of the times and religious dictates. Perhaps All Hallows Eve or Hallowmas would have remained a vehicle for various sects of the European Christian religion to offer prayers for their dead and a celebration for the peasantry to enjoy the last of the harvest season, if it had not been for two historical events that we'll cover when we finally touch down in the American Halloween airport. Ironically, the church gave the holiday its name, sanctioning the long-standing custom of remembering the dead, adding credence to the parades, feasts, bonfires, and masquerades, and creating much of the beloved symbolism we use in our modern Halloween celebrations, though this symbolism was created to frighten, rather than entertain, the public.

Every culture creates customs for human death that include acts of honor and the concept of immortality. The original Samhain gave the early Paleopagans a way to deal with the mystery of dying. Today, we are still trying to understand the basic concept of life, and the nature of death. If we learn anything from studying the history of Halloween, it is that ancient peoples (regardless of race or culture) believed that death does not kill. Although the early church would have been delighted to destroy Samhain, they were forced to accept the holiday and used the celebration to meet the needs of the political and social structure of the time. In the New World Halloween would find strong purchase, despite the misgivings of the church, and become a holiday separate from religious mythos and political tyranny.

The Silver 2000 has begun its descent into the American Halloween. Those of you who wish to remain on this flight, kindly keep your boarding passes with you as you disembark. You will need to show them to the attendant when you reenter the broom for our flight to the modern Halloween.

The American Halloween

Holidays, as I'm sure you've guessed by now, are often at the mercy of the governing religious and political bodies of the times. By the 1630s the word "Samhain" was lost somewhere in antiquity, crushed under the hard heel of the authorities of the Christian Church, political and personal struggle, wars, pestilence, and famine. We've also discovered that harvest celebrations do not belong to one particular religious persuasion, nor does the act of honoring the dead belong to any single religious body.

Our first inkling of Halloween coming to America revolves not around a specific set of people (many indicate the Irish), as several researchers have supposed, but with the compendium of individuals entering America and the establishment of the various colonies. Let's peek in on some of these colonies and see what's happening. We have to be careful that the Puritans don't see us, though—we certainly wouldn't want to land our broom there!

Short Hop to Virginia

I've never quite understood why we give the Puritans so much credit when the first settlers of America bumped into the area we know as Virginia in 1607. Settlers from England, Germany, Poland, France, and Scotland ventured here, along with a large population of Africans (whom we realize were not brought to Virginia by choice). Government and practices of society evolved from an English-style hierarchy, pulling the Anglican Church to the forefront of religious choice in this colony. The Anglican Church finds its roots in the Catholic belief system when, in the sixteenth century, Henry VIII came into conflict with Rome (interesting that a change in church structure should come about because a king can't decide which wife to keep; perhaps Henry should have accepted polygamy, rather than kill off the ladies!). Although Protestant, the church kept much of its Catholic background, including the doctrine, liturgy, and organization. Henry's daughter, Elizabeth I, promised to blend Protestant and Catholic elements. Although the Anglicans threw out the saints, they kept All Saints' Day as a feast day and All Souls' Day as an unofficial holy day.[27]

Colonial life in Virginia kept the folk beliefs in the spirit world as well as the practices of astrology, palmistry, the throwing of lots, and other divination procedures. The Christian religion and magickal sciences/religious structure were not separate as they are today, though the colonial government frowned on such practices and instituted a few laws to dissuade believers. Early Virginian estate libraries commonly held books on alchemy, astrology, various healing practices, German occultism, Hermeticism, and Rosicrucian practices.

Virginians celebrated numerous fairs throughout September and October that included judging and selling horses, sheep, hogs, cows, oxen, chickens, homemade products, contests, games, puppet shows, races, bonfires, and fortunetelling. Not only did the harvest festivals bring excitement and fun to the people, they also (with the support of the Anglican Church) gave official status, through All Souls' Day and All Saints' Day, to honoring the dead.

A Tour of Colonial Pennsylvania

We have additional support for the American Halloween with William Penn's motley collection of refugees from Europe. In 1683, Penn wrote a promotional tract inviting dissatisfied Europeans to come and relish the freedom of Penn's Woods (Pennsylvania). Consequently, fifty ships dropped their anchors in the Delaware River. They discharged persecuted souls from England, Ireland, Wales, and the Rhineland (now Germany). In all, 2,500 people came to Philadelphia and occupied 350 houses on those first brave ships. The highest percentage of these individuals were German, and wave upon wave of additional German settlers entered America throughout 1700–1799. A second Irish wave hit America in 1720, many settling along the Appalachian mountains. Collectively, the Germans and Irish share Celtic heritage; therefore, many of their folk customs resonated together, including Halloween observances and local harvest celebrations.

With the Quaker rule of religious tolerance that lasted until 1756, Halloween flourished under the auspices of the German and Irish settlements. A high percentage of the Germans were Lutheran (leaving Catholicism) but they still celebrated the saints' days as well as All Souls' Day. Pennsylvania also supported German Catholics, Moravians, Roman Catholics, and other small sects (including the strong presence of a group of Presbyterian Scotch-Irish settlers), which helped keep alive the colorful harvest festivals and the practice of honoring the dead.

Pennsylvania, perhaps more than any other colony, reveled in all sorts of folk magick. As early as 1694, German mystic Johannes Kelpius established a settlement near Philadelphia that recognized astrology, Hermeticism, and other psychic and spiritual endeavors, helping to keep the celebration of Halloween alive and well.

The Other Colonies

Maryland welcomed Catholic refugees. In 1649, Maryland's Act of Toleration officially gave freedom of conscience to Roman Catholics, Puritans, and Quakers. Unfortunately, the Puritans overthrew the government and prosecuted the Catholics. In 1688, the Puritans were ousted and the colony returned to English rule and the Anglican Church, and therefore supported the harvest celebrations and days for the dead. We should keep in mind that if the Puritans had succeeded in their plan of overtaking all the governments of the colonies, then Halloween and many of the other holidays we celebrate today would not be part of our American culture. Only North Carolina, South Carolina, and Georgia have celebrated an uninterrupted observance of both harvest festivals and recognition of days for the dead.

Early American Halloween

From 1684 through 1845, Halloween was considered a local function tied either to your religious persuasion or to your community social structure. Two Halloween practices surfaced that would become the forerunners of our modern American Halloween: Mischief Night and community parties.

Many of the tricks in the German, Scotch, and Irish communities became universal, such as overturning outhouses, dismantling a wagon on the ground and putting it back together on top of a house or barn, and tying cows to church bells. The tricks often served as a social function, such as mildly chastising a neighbor who exhibited antisocial behavior. Although some historians believe that Mischief Night is a direct result of Guy Fawkes Day in England, we can see that such a holiday would have little effect on the German, Scotch, or Irish communities.

On Mischief Night, "children are half under the impression that lawlessness is permissible. Householder's front doors are repeatedly assaulted with bogus calls, the gates removed, the dustbin lids hoisted up lamp posts, their window panes daubed with paint, and their doorknobs coated with treacle."[28] Chalking circles on clothing and later, designs on walkways, became an exciting endeavor for neighborhood children.

Community parties danced across America, celebrating the family as well as the holiday. From mid-October to early November, various towns, hamlets, and farming communities found celebration in the harvest of agricultural goods, the joy of a good foot-stomping barn dance, and the wonderful shakes and quivers created by the theatrical telling of a heart-stopping ghost tale.

Whether we are discussing All Hallows Eve, Snap Apple Night, or the Nut Crack Night, we have the beginnings of a mutually accepted holiday, regardless of one's religious preference. Although not the Halloween we know quite yet, these celebrations and acts of mischief are the direct catalyst for our American Halloween. Between 1820 and 1870, nearly 7.4 million people entered America from countries all over the world. Every group had a folk magick tradition, and each had an impact on the folk traditions of America. As Halloween celebrations grew, each culture added to the magickal compendium of the holiday. Non-European peoples, such as the African Americans and Spanish Catholics from neighboring Mexico, added their magick and beliefs to Halloween too.[29] Let's broom further into the future and see what disaster (the potato famine) helped to firmly entrench Halloween in the United States.

The Great Potato Famine of Ireland

From 1845 to 1847, the already oppressed citizens of Ireland suffered a disastrous famine that resulted in the failure of the potato crop. Large numbers of people from Ireland, Scotland, Britain, and Germany immigrated to the United States. From 1841 to 1850, over 1,713,000 of these people entered America, solidifying the earlier Celtic invasions. These people brought with them their family unity, religious persuasion, and folk customs, including their Halloween practices. Many of these individuals settled first in Boston, New York, Baltimore, and Philadelphia, then joined the western migration. Of particular interest in our search for the American Halloween is the Irish custom in which groups of girls gathered together at midnight on Halloween to perform their secret divinations with apples, fire, mirrors, and yarn. We'll cover some of these techniques in our divination chapter. However, we must be going before those giggling girls catch sight of us. Trying to explain time travel at this point would be a bit difficult. May I see your boarding passes, please? We're off to the Victorian Halloween—I will warn you, however, proper dress is required!

The Victorian Halloween

As the industrial revolution hit America, so did the urge to return to a simpler time. Halloween made its debut in the upper crust of American society in the early 1870s, interpreted by the well-to-do social structure as a quaint, entertaining English practice. Rich Protestants especially did not want to recognize its Catholic influences, but were more than happy to celebrate anything that may have come from northern England. Books, newspapers, and magazine articles of the times reflected an inaccurate historical background for the holiday, which helped the growth of the celebration. It is around this time as previously noted that someone made up the Samhain Celtic God of the Dead, and this misinformation continues through into our current culture. Remember, the Samhain Lord who judged the dead and sentenced sinning souls did not exist in the Celtic culture.[30]

To the Victorian Americans (both upper and middle class), the need to remove the association with the dead, WitchCraft, sacrifices, offerings, and destruction was essential. Printed material of the times concentrated on entertaining games, parties, and other fun activities. It was okay, however, to communicate with the dead for one's romantic interests, and this practice grew in popularity, especially with the young people. Victorian editors peddled the deliciously mysterious rather than the grave-ful dead. High-society matrons used the season to hold costumed balls and parties for charitable ventures; however, it was felt that Halloween was only for the young as an excuse for matchmaking, and a holiday that married couples would have no interest in.

We've landed in the year of 1890 and, as we walk through the streets, we see that many magazines and newspapers commonly carry articles on how to give a proper Halloween party, divination games, designing invitations, carving jack-o'-lanterns, recipes, and other assorted novelties. (The two ladies over there . . . see them? They're talking about how they are planning to make a match of Abagail and Huford. I hope they like each other because they'll be married by spring if these ladies have any say in the matter!) The Victorians did much to remove the significant historical value of the holiday and, by the time they were through, the celebrations of the times were considered part of a "new" holiday. Soon, though, the Victorian matchmaking parties would become passé (guess those matches didn't work out well after all) and the children of America would lay claim to the holiday.

We are now boarding the Silver 2000. We have one more stop before our final destination. Please remember to take your snack out of the compartment by the loading door and take it with you to your seat.

An American Halloween in the Twentieth Century

By 1910, several American manufacturers were making or importing party products just for the new American holiday of Halloween. From noisemakers to costumes, a new holiday meant increased business, which, of course, means the opportunity to make money. With the increased focus on children, the divination, matchmaking, and kissing games fell to the wayside as American parents felt such things inappropriate for children's consumption. The first Halloween parades organized in American were in Anoka, Minnesota, and Allentown, Pennsylvania, in 1921. Floats, marching bands, and costumed townspeople marched through history and, with the communication network of newspapers, sent a flurry of public celebrations across America. The advent of the Halloween parade solidified Halloween in American community activities.

The drawback to the new holiday came in the form of the "declared" Mischief Night, Goblin Night, or Devil's Night on October 30, mentioned earlier. Most of the pranks were harmless, but things did manage to get out of hand. In Dillsburg, Pennsylvania, the German hometown boys stole four outhouses, bales of hay, and corn shocks, setting each outhouse on a corner of the town square, blocking all entrances to the town. In another instance, the boys of the town took a huge wagon and perched it atop a barn. Minor offenses, such as tying several garbage cans together and hanging them from a light pole to soaping windows with lard (and later, bars of hand soap) abounded. As the pranks grew to vandalism, the shopkeepers and store owners would bribe youngsters to ward off destruction of their property.

Unfortunately, militant groups took advantage of these Mischief Nights, and records indicate that the Ku Klux Klan enacted horrendous crimes during this period, hiding under the guise of Mischief Night. In 1925, the Chicago Principals' Club started a highly organized campaign to alter criminal behavior, encouraging students and parents to demonstrate their responsibility by cleaning up yards, fixing fences, and performing other charitable labors. Those children who participated in these events were rewarded with parties from local adult clubs, such as the Kiwanis, Lions, and Rotarians. In an effort to stop the criminal behavior, the Boy Scouts, in conjunction with local councils of towns, cities, and boroughs, instituted the custom of Trick-or-Treating Night to keep youngsters from naughty practices and pull the power of Mischief Night out of the hands of the Ku Klux Klan. By the 1930s, the custom of trick-or-treating was well entrenched in our American culture. Halloween, like Christmas, became a holiday for children, and parents strove to make the holiday as much fun as possible for the enjoyment of their youngsters—but the major problems with vandalism were far from over.

In 1938, the commissioner of police in Boston paid for ice cream and cake at various parties in fifteen district police stations to keep the mischief at a minimum but, despite the valiant attempts of various community groups and organizations, Mischief Night was still a problem. In 1939 in Queens, New York, 1,000 windows were broken. By 1940, many towns, cities, and boroughs decided to eliminate Halloween activities, but it was World War II that would bring public awareness to a new level.

World War II Halloween

"Letting the air out of tires isn't fun anymore. It's sabotage. Soaping windows isn't fun this year. Your government needs soap and greases for the war. Carting away property isn't fun this year. You may be taking something intended for scrap, or something that can't be replaced because of war shortages. Even ringing doorbells has lost its appeal because it may mean disturbing the sleep of a tired war worker who needs his rest," wrote James M. Spinning, superintendent of schools in Rochester, New York, in 1942.[31] Civic groups, local governments, newspapers, radio, school districts, and magazine publishers joined forces to eliminate the vandalism of Mischief Night during the war years, preaching to the public how destructive these practices could be to the "American Cause." Although some communities cancelled Halloween celebrations during the Second World War, many used the holiday as an excuse to boost public morale, believing there was a real need for recreational activities to level war fears. Ideas for costumes and parties were adjusted so as not to deplete the country's resources. As patriotic devotion ran high, vandalism dipped to all-time lows.

Halloween: The Last Fifty Years

With the war over, communities and civic groups returned to their campaigns for a safe Halloween. Parades were reinstituted and community activities picked up their pace. Halloween practices now extended through the entire month of October, not just Trick-or-Treating Night (which often does not fall on the original Halloween Eve, in a community effort to make the holiday safe for roaming children). Events sponsored by businesses, town councils, church organizations, charity groups, and private individuals were held throughout the month in the form of haunted houses, parties, hay rides, plays, story hours, and numerous other events. Participatory numbers of children and adults involved in the holiday jumped to amazing levels and Halloween's popularity rivaled the celebrations of the Fourth of July and Memorial Day.

The Halloween Battle

In the mid to late 1990s, certain sects of the Protestant Christian Church declared war on Halloween, using the same erroneous propaganda cultivated hundreds of years ago by their Catholic predecessors. Other groups seized Halloween for their own political agendas, sponsoring haunted houses showing aborted babies, drug addicts, and other modern-day violent situations. This did not go over well, as the holiday had moved to an event primarily for children, not for adult political issues. Radical Christian groups said that the holiday was Satanic—which, as we've seen from our research, is a bizarre and fantastic claim based on misinformation, politicking, personal agendas, and fear, not fact. Keep in mind that radical Christians tried to do the same thing with Christmas around the turn of the century, which didn't work.

With America's separation policy of church and state, the battle for destroying Halloween in the United States is an uphill one and does not promise a successful outcome. With our country's diverse population, myriad cultures, and growing variety in religious choice, one single religion may attempt to, but cannot ultimately, hold prisoner any cross-cultural holiday for its own agenda. What is important, however, is how this type of attack has historically changed the way we do things, because the radical rebellion against Halloween by various political factions will alter, in some respect, the way we celebrate the holiday. The Satanic Panic instituted by these "godly" people has caused serious aggression against innocent individuals. Sociologists believe that this need to control through fear is the platform of Satanic Panic, which indicates low self-esteem, the desire for ultimate control of the environment, and the fear of that which is unknown or uncontrollable.

It is amusing that these fanatical factions have campaigned to put the "harvest" back in Halloween, urging their followers to practice harvest-like celebrations, rather than the American Halloween. Isn't that what the holiday was in the first place? Perhaps they are going back to Pagan roots, after all.

Halloween Murder

We've all heard the horror stories of poisoned candy or apples stuffed with razor blades. From 1950 through 1960, our American Halloween customs stayed primarily the same. The sixties encouraged something "new"—Halloween safety—and as a result magazines, newspapers, television, and radio were filled with a compendium of ideas on how to keep your child safe and have an enjoyable Halloween, a campaign that has remained up to the present time. Manufacturers jumped into "safe" costumes and "safe" decorations that met "safety" standards.

In the early 1970s, a candy scare put a major dent in everyone's Halloween budget. In the past, even if you didn't have a lot of money, you could make cookies, zap up popcorn balls, buy a bushel of apples, or wrap homemade candy to give to the little critters that came to your door. Your bank account was not devastated and the children were happy. In 1970, all this changed. Kevin Tostan, a five-year-old boy, allegedly ate Halloween candy laced with heroin. Mothers and fathers of America whooped a battle cry, but investigators discovered that the heroin belonged to the boy's uncle and was not a Halloween treat. Then, on Halloween 1974, Timothy O'Bryan, eight years of age, died of cyanide poisoning after eating a supposed Halloween treat. The father, Ronald Clark O'Bryan, claimed that the boy had gotten the candy from a house in Pasadena, Texas. Nothing is ever as it seems, and so it was with this unfortunate death. The house in question was empty Halloween Eve and authorities discovered that the father had taken out a $20,000 life insurance policy on each of his children, and that he had poisoned his own son. He also attempted to poison his daughter.

Ronald O'Bryan was sentenced to death by injection to occur on Halloween 1982, but received a stay of execution.

A survey by sociologist Joel Best at California State University in Fresno found that in nearly thirty years, not a single death or severe injury was caused by a Halloween sadist,[32] yet Halloween hysteria still exists and manages to dampen our Halloween fun. Horror stories of razor blades in apples, drugs in Halloween candy, and adults dressed in strange costumes so that they may first frighten and then murder their unsuspecting prey have evolved into the urban legend—things that aren't true, but could be, so maybe they are. Sociologists believe that the national trend toward prohibition as a ready answer for *any* problem is really a signal that adults feel they have lost control over the next generation. Further, some sociologists feel that the new customs of emphasizing these urban legends and arguing against Halloween activities are nothing but "preemptive narrative acts of aggression against the young generation."[33] Gee, and you thought goblins and ghouls were scary!

Halloween is Healthy

Halloween can be scary for some children as well as adults.

> According to child psychologist, Dr. Lee Salk, such fears are normal, and Halloween is a good time for kids to deal with them. Halloween allows anxieties and misgivings to come out into the open, letting children manage what is at other times nightmarish. It is a time that helps them deal with any fears of death, darkness, ghosts, and monsters openly, without the risk of being laughed at by their peers or adults. Dr. Salk explains, "Halloween today has a special significance because many children feel helpless in the face of violence on television, kidnappings, and other tragedies occurring in their world. So today the monsters under the bed that scare them are really the monsters inside their heads." Since Halloween is actually a publicly endorsed chance to be outrageous, it allows the child to become the "monster" of his or her fears.[34]

This psychology applies to adults as well. The older we get, the more experience we accumulate, the greater our fears. Like children, some adults are affected by these fears more than others. By watching a scary movie in a dark living room while dipping our fingers into homemade buttery popcorn, or snuggling under mounds of covers and fluffy propped pillows in bed with your favorite Stephen King novel, or going all-out for Halloween, we are subconsciously attacking our fears so that we can live normal, productive lives. If your child shows fear at a particular costume, urge him or her to find solace in the fantasy and magick of Halloween. Stay away from the costumes that scare him or her (especially the morbid or gross ones for the little kids). You never know, though—even Santa Claus has the habit of scaring the diapers right off of some little children, so be extra observant and attune yourself to your child's needs.

"Any Halloween?"—Halloween Collectibles

The autumn months, say Dan and Pauline Campanelli of Flying Witch Farm,[35] are the best time to find those great Halloween collectibles at flea markets and antique shops, but if you are very nice and pop your head in the door asking, "Any Halloween?" you're apt to find all sorts of goodies the whole year 'round. Unlike other collectibles, Halloween pieces aren't relegated to one type of material. They range from cardboard, papier-mâché, tin, glass, cloth, wax, wood, ceramic, and more. There are so many types of Halloween decorations that you may choose to specialize in just one category or a single time period. As with all collectibles, price is tricky. The old adage "one man's prize is another man's junk" can apply; however, Halloween treasures top out at a little less than a thousand dollars, with a high number of pieces ranging from a worth of thirty dollars to three hundred and fifty. A paperback book entitled *Egyptian Witch Fortune Teller and Dream Book,* published by Behrens Publishing Company in Danbury, Connecticut, sold for a quarter in 1874. Today, its market value is thirty-five dollars. By looking at the publishing date and the contents of the book, historically we know that in the late 1800s fortunetelling during Halloween festivities in America was present, but there is something deeper here—who held the book? Who giggled uproariously as they read the fortunes to amaze their friends? Perhaps ambiance was added—apple cinnamon pie in the oven and a candle positioned in the center of mama's large, round kitchen table, the smell of harvest in the fields as father opened the kitchen door . . . whispered fortunes carried on the wind?

Many of the first noise makers and tin, cardboard, and plaster pumpkin and cat decorations were imported from Germany as the 1800s became history and consumer demand pushed Halloween into the bright new dawn of the twentieth century. Many of these stunning pieces were made by hand and the artwork is exceptional. Some of America's best known and most loved artists designed seasonal magazine covers, including Norman Rockwell and his stunning Halloween renditions for the *Saturday Evening Post*. Paper dolls, post cards, advertisements, placecards, and posters can tell us more of America's celebration of Halloween and holiday art history than any timeline, book, movie, or impromptu speech. When you see these items there is a quick surprise, a rush of memory, the joy of something you have lost and now found. "I remember that!" tumbles from your lips as you gaze at a long-forgotten image from your childhood and discover that maybe, just maybe, you're not so insulated by modern technology that you have forgotten the simple pleasures of the past. That warm and pleasant memory, after all, is priceless.

Summary

The original Samhain marked the close of the season and now functions as the third and final harvest festival in the Pagan year (Lughnasadh is the first harvest festival, occurring in August; Fall Equinox is the second harvest festival and falls in September; Samhain is the third celebration, occurring in October). In America, Halloween has become the first holiday in our end-of-year rush for party gaiety. Our Halloween functions as the opening of a three-month-long celebratory fest that includes Thanksgiving, Christmas, Yule, Kwanza, and Hanukah, to name just a few, and ends with the popular American New Year.

The American Halloween became a cultural celebration rather than a religious one. Our children carve pumpkins with delightful chatter and adults find solace in a night where they can be whatever they want to be. We have little doubt about the joy this holiday brings to the American people. We will forever love the haunted house, the vampire costume, the harvest moon, the thrills and chills of a well-wrought ghostly tale—and, of course, the deliciously scary things that go EEEEK in the night!

Notes

1. "Paleopaganism refers to the original tribal faiths of Europe, Africa, Asia, the Americas, Oceania and Australia, when they were (or in some cases, still are) practiced as intact belief systems." Isaac Bonewitz, "Defining Paganism: Paleo-, Meso-, and Neo- 2.1" at www.neopagan.net.

2. Jean Markale, *The Celts*, Inner Traditions, 1978, page 25.

3. Isaac Bonewits, "Indo-European Paleopaganism and Its Clergy, 1.5," www.neopagan.net.

4. Ibid.

5. W. J. Bethancourt III, "Halloween: Myths, Monsters and Devils" www.geocities.com/Athens/Delphi/6696/hallows.htm. This is the best site on the web for scholarly debunking of erroneous Halloween tales.

6. Rowan Moonstone, "The Origins of Halloween," at www.geocities.com/Athens/Delphi/6696/rowan.htm. This can also be found in tract form originating from Colorado Springs, 1989, CultWatch Response.

7. Mike Nichols, "The Witches' Sabbats," 1986, www.geocities.com/Athens/Forum/7280/samhain.html. Mike has an excellent selection of information on his site for all eight Pagan holidays.

8. Bethancourt.

9. To learn more about the faeries, contact Elvendrums@aol.com or visit their website at members.aol.com/elvendrums or write them a letter at Elvendrums, P. O. Box 105751, Jefferson City, MO 65110-5751.

   According to faery expert Devan, "They say that those who had danced in the land of the sidhe with the faer (sic) folk pined away for the music forever; if they returned, the humans thought the music was simple, but soon discovered that the tunes were impossibly complex to reproduce. To play like a faery was the ultimate compliment."

10. "The name druid (Irish drui, Welsh derwydd) is derived from the Sanskrit root veda, to see or know, and is also associated with the oak (Irish daur, Welsh derw, and Gaulish dervo). The druidic task was a shamanic one, requiring a deep and encyclopedic knowledge of many branches of wisdom, art and science, and an ability to interrelate the many dimensions of the otherworld. Druids, both male and female, acted as the counselors, philosophers, shapeshifters, diviners and magicians of the rulers."

11. Ross Nichols, *The Book of Druidry*, Thorsons, 1990. "What remained and was cultivated was wisdom, mystic quarterings, and sun and moon observances, often put into poems; but this becomes complicated by Greek culture. The Celtic Druids knew Greek writing from about 600 B.C., and the Druid Abaris, mentioned by Diodorus Siculus, is recorded as speaking Greek perfectly."

12. Lyn Webster Wilde, *Celtic Women in Legend, Myth and History*, Sterling Publishing Company, 1997.

13. Ibid.

14. Caitlin and John Matthews, *The Encyclopedia of Celtic Wisdom*, Element Books, 1994. "The overlap of local indigenous shamanic tradition and official druidic practice is difficult to judge in Britain and Ireland. We hear of the Nemedian druid, Miach, overcoming the indigenous 'druids.' "

15. Bethancourt.

16. John Greenway, *Folklore of the Great West*, American West Publishing Co., 1970, page 384.

17. Margaret Murray, *Witchcult in Western Europe*.

18. Wilde.

19. Julio CaroBaroja, *World of Witches*, University of Chicago Press, 1961.

20. Rossel Hope Robbins, *Encyclopedia of Witchcraft and Demonology*, Crown Publishers, 1959.

21. Hroch, Miroslave and Anna Skybova, Ecclesia Militans—The Inquisition, Dorset Press, Germany, 1988, page 11.

22. Christina Hole, *Witchcraft in England*, Charles Scribner's Sons, 1947; Ewen C. L'Estange, *Witch Hunting and Witch Trials*, Dial Press, 1929.

23. Robbins, page 551.

24. J. N. D. Kelly, *The Oxford Dictionary of Popes*, Oxford University Press, 1986.

25. Matthews. "By now there was a great fear of ghosts, the souls who returned to their homes and refused to go upon their tuirgen (spirit walk). The feast of Samhain, held in honor of dead ancestors, was bound about with precautions so that the stray souls of the recently dead should not be attracted but sent quickly on their way. In Christian times, prayers for the dead are said for the repose of such souls. Lanterns are still set in windows to guide lost souls. A corpse and its possessions were not allowed to remain long in mortal places. The deceased's bedding was taken to the fairy mounds or burned. (This practice was kept in, of all places, Pennsylvania Dutch practices until the mid-twentieth century.)"

26. Bethancourt.

27. For information about Henry VIII shenanigans, see the following resources: Rossel Hope Robbins, *Encyclopedia of Witchcraft and Demonology*, Crown Publishers, 1959; Ewen C. L'Estange, *Witch Hunting and Witch Trials*, Dial Press, 1929; and Barbara Rosen, *Witchcraft*, Stratford-Upon-Avon Library, 1969.

28. Iona and Peter Opie, *The Lore and Language of School Children*, Claredon Press, 1959, page 276.

29. Lesley Pratt Bannatyne, *Halloween: An American Holiday*, Facts on File, Inc., 1990, page 53.

30. Over the next thirty years, Episcopal All Saints' Day celebrations grew more public and more popular. Although the Catholic Church celebrated All Saints' Day in accordance with its years of history and heritage, it simply did not receive as much acknowledgment in the press. As a result, vast numbers of American readers came to understand All Saints' Day as Episcopalian in origin.

31. "Hits Halloween Revels," *New York Times*, October 23, 1942, page 16.

32. Joel Best, "The Razor Blade in the Apple: The Social Construction of Urban Legends," *Social Problems*, Volume 32, No. 5, June 1985, pages 448–449.

33. Ibid.

34. Meridith Brokaw and Annie Gilbar, *The Penny Whistle Halloween Book*, Simon & Schuster, 1991, page 9.

35. Dan and Pauline Campanelli, *Halloween Collectables—A Price Guide*, L-W Book Sales, 1995.

Velinda held the flickering light
And cast grim shadows on the wall
While whispering stories in my ear
On Halloween so long ago.

The ghosts she conjured howled then
To match the winds that moaned outside,
Her Witches crossed the golden moon
On brooms above the clouds they'd ride.

That night I'd try my best to sleep
With thoughts of graveyards in my mind
I'd pull the covers o'er my head
To leave those visions far behind.

Now she's living in New Hampshire,
Over forty years have passed us by
Still, on Halloween, I hear her whisper
And once again the Witches fly!

—© 1998 DAVID O. NORRIS,
"HALLOWEEN 1953"

chapter 2

HALLOWEEN CUSTOMS AND TRADITIONS

*C*ome with me
All Hallow's night
We'll frighten everyone in sight
Such pranks, for once,
are justified
And fun and frolic amplified.

—FROM AN EARLY NINETEENTH-CENTURY
HALLOWEEN POSTCARD

37

Much of society, from Paleopagan times through the early 1900s, was centered around the festivals of Halloween, Christmas, Easter, and the occasional fair or other community activity (such as a national holiday). What else was there, really, to do? Most people didn't have much money, and a large percentage of the world's population was occupied with farming endeavors and the basic act of survival. These special days carried a sense of excitement that grew through the preparations and reached a crescendo of joy and laughter through family and community functions. In the fall, vegetables were carved, breads were baked, costumes were fussed over, and fires or candles were lit for the dead. Halloween was a time to overeat, tell jokes, gossip with the gang, drink too much, do a little fortunetelling and, finally, to have a wonderful time scaring the stuffing out of everyone with scary stories and tales of the mysterious and unexplained. Whether we are talking about the year of 1511, when breads were baked and delivered for all Christian souls,[1] or into the twenty-first century, where a variety of popular movie or television cartoon characters roam the night, Halloween was historically a time to summon happiness, batten down the hatches for the winter ahead, and create a sense of childlike wonder in the conjuration of that-which-we-don't-understand.

The Jack-o'-Lantern

Pumpkins smiling, pumpkins leering, fun pumpkins, sad pumpkins, mean pumpkins, exotic pumpkins—where did this fascination come from? We certainly can't have Halloween without our friend the pumpkin.

The centerpiece of the American Halloween tradition is the jack-o'-lantern—the gutted pumpkin carved with a delightful design that glows by the insertion of a candle or battery-operated light. Many historians in our century claim that the original idea for the jack-o'-lantern came from the Celts, who hollowed out apples and vegetables (even turnips) and used them as safe candle holders, which were later used by medieval Europeans as small lanterns. Whether or not the early Celts carved faces in the apples, turnips, or beets to ward off evil is debatable. Have you ever tried to carve a turnip? It ain't easy. The pumpkin is an American vegetable, and therefore the pumpkin-carving fun you experience today belongs on the long list of American inventions. A background check on carving faces to scare away evil, ghosts, Witches, and black cats shows us that the early Celts did not believe in Witches, they had no cats, and they liked the ghosts of their ancestors. With the insistence of the Christian church to attach all Pagan-related practices to negative superstition, it is hard to determine just why faces were carved in the vegetables, if at all.

Mysterious, eerie lights that appeared floating in the Halloween fog, bobbing along on the crest of the marshes and swamps, were called will-o'-the-wisps, corpse candles, lantern men, hob-o'-lanterns, jack-o'-lanterns, or, simply, will. Scientifically we know that these unusual manifestations are a product of *ignis fatuus* (foolish fire) created by decaying matter that releases a spontaneous, combustible gas; however, the unexplainable has always led to spectacular folk tales, and in the case of the jack-o'-lantern, the physical creation of the hollowed-out turnip, beet, or pumpkin depicting the face of a skull came to be an added bonus in the storytelling! In Scotland, the carved turnips are called "bogies," and in England, the hollowed beets are "punkies." So just think—you can tell the PTA this year that you are bringing punkies and bogies for the children's party. Some of you may look at the turnips in the grocery store and think, "That's not big enough to carve." I can truly tell you that the turnips and beets in my garden last year grew as large as a small pumpkin—too tough to eat, but perfect for that Samhain fest!

Folklorists have not been able to pinpoint the birth of the tale of Jack and his frightening lantern, and several renditions can be found in historical interview accounts, popular books on Halloween, and even on the Internet. It is believed that the story is European driven, easing into America as various immigrants crossed the waters to their new home. The theme of the story appears to have Christian roots (or at least was Christianized at some point), as the significant antagonist is the devil (who did not romp through original Celtic mythos). I have given you my version of the story here:

Once upon a time there was farmer by the name of Jack. He wasn't an unlikable fellow, no he wasn't, but he was the sort of fella that would run from honest work faster than a youngin' can run from bath water. Tall and lanky, Jack had a lopsided smile and a missin' tooth. A nice laugh—one that rumbled deep from the belly and danced about the barn quicker than a fellow with a fiddle in his hand. His hair was limp and his face was creased—yep, that was our Jack all right.

One fine day, the devil . . . well, he got bored. Temptin' the rich folk got far too easy, so he set out to find hisself a poor boy. That old devil, he spied Jack sleepin' under the big old oak tree out there by the garden. "Jack," he says, "I've come to take your soul."

"If'n you can climb that oak tree and touch the top, then you kin have it," said Jack. "Ain't no never-mind to me."

Ain't no one in the county able to climb to the top of that big ole tree, and Jack, well . . . he knew that, yes he did.

So the devil, he climbs the tree, but he gets stuck and cain't git down. "Jack, help me down," says the devil.

"Nope," says Jack, "because if'n I do, you'll want to take my soul. If'n you stay in that tree, you cain't git me."

Now the devil, he thinks and thinks, and then he says, "If'n you help me down, I'll give you anythin' you want. Just name it."

Jack walks around the tree, lookin' up at the devil from different angles. He scratches his beard and cocks his head. "Okay," says Jack, "If'n I let you down, you have to promise me that you'll never allow me into hell."

"Done!" says the devil, and Jack helps him down.

"Well now," thought Jack, "this is mighty fine, I kin do as I please!" And so he did. Poor Jack. Nobody believe his story, so he took to drinkin' and then to gamblin' and I hear tell he coveted the wife of a neighbor man, and ran off with another—I ain't rightly sure. Anyway, Jack finally up and died.

Well now, Jack went to heaven and stood in front of them pearly gates and the angel there said, "You cain't come in here. We's only got room for good people, and Jack, you weren't so good down there on earth. I'm afraid you'll have to go to the other place."

Jack stood in front of the gates of hell, but the demon said, "Sorry Jack, you cain't come in here. You made a deal with the devil. There's no room at this end unless, of course, you can exchange your soul for another's."

"But it's dark down here and I cain't see," said Jack. "How will I find someone to take my place?"

"Here," said the demon, and threw Jack a glowing coal.

Now Jack, he wasn't a stupid fellow, so he took hisself a turnip outta the garden and hollowed it out, then put that hot coal in the turnip so's he could see, as the world of in-between is mighty dark. On Halloween night, when the veil between the worlds is thin, you kin see Jack and his little light, across the fields and in the woods, roamin' in the night, searchin' for someone to take his place.

Now, if you hollow out that there turnip, and put a candle in it, then Jack will think you're lost too, and he won't pay you no never mind. He never was a really smart fella.

The traditional jack-o'-lantern takes a strange twist in southern America, in such states as Mississippi and Louisiana, where African American lore collided with European legend. Jack's story takes on a different twist here, and he is described as a sort of gnome or goblin (much like the southern version of a pookha). A cross between a dog, a human, and a cartoon character, this munchkin has sports-goggle eyes, sausage lips, and is covered in fur. This Jack was swift of foot and could outrun the fastest horse in the country.[2]

Today, pumpkin carving has turned into an art form of its own with national contests, exotic designs, and even special tools. We've got pumpkin scoopers, pumpkin saws, and way-cool pumpkin patterns to launch any Halloween party or trick-or-treating extravaganza. And pumpkins are far easier to carve than turnips!

Trick-or-Treating Night

Soul! soul! Or a soul cake;

Pray, good mistress, for a soul cake.

One for Peter, two for Paul

Three for them that made us all.

Soul! Soul! Or an apple or two;

If you've got no apples, pears will do.

Up with your kettle, and down with your pan

Give me a good big one, and I'll be gone.

Soul! Soul! Or a soul cake;

An apple or pear, a plum or a cherry,

Is a very good thing to make us merry.

Soul! Soul! Or a soul cake.[3]

We can find the original source of trick-or-treating in the Celtic practice of leaving special food as an offering to the dead, much like the Mexican *ofrenda*. The practice of going from house to house is not a new one at all, and isn't just for Halloween. While doing research on New Year's Day for Llewellyn's *1999 Witches Calendar*, I found several references, both European and American, that indicate house to house visits for various holidays occurred often. Halloween, then, is not an exception, but represents the rule of both Pagan and early Christian holiday revelry. House-begging on Halloween became the norm throughout the original Celtic territories. Some historical accounts say that only children practiced house-begging, but other references indicate that adults participated as well. It is from these house to house visits, involving laughter, song, and general revelry, that we have the birth of the American practice of trick-or-treating, the American Halloween parade, and costuming for both of these events.

The most eminent folklorist to date on the subject of Halloween is John Santino, who has spent several years studying both European and American practices and legends associated with this holiday. His most recent work traces the European act of "rhyming" (going from house to house) and "mumming" as the precursor to the

American version of trick-or-treating. When researching any facet of Halloween practices, yesterday or today, we discover that traditions are highly localized and vary from region to region, town to town, village to village, and city block to city block. [4]

Adults and children who practiced rhyming went from house to house, usually before Halloween (sometimes up to a full month before), knocking on doors and then giving some sort of performance including a rhyme. In many areas of Ireland, the payment for such entertainment was in the form of money, where in Britain and Germany we find the gift of food (the soul cake, apples, or other edible pastries and perhaps, if you were good, a cup of fresh buttermilk). If you came to the door too soon, you were sent away and had to wait a week or two. The favored rhyme for this occasion in Ireland was:

Hallowe'en is coming on and the geese are getting fat.
Will you please put a penny in the old lad's hat?
If you haven't got a penny, a ha' penny will do.
If you haven't got a ha' penny, a farthing will do.
If you haven't got a farthing, then a piece of bread will do.
If you haven't got a piece of bread, God bless you, and your old lad, too.

(Meaning if you didn't even have a crust of bread, you were certainly in bad shape, and you needed all the prayers you could get.)

Mumming, which is the precursor of the Halloween parade, appears to be a bit more complicated, including costuming and additional choreography. Somewhere along the historical line, Halloween rhyming and Christmas mumming managed to blend to the point where accounts cited by individuals now in their eighties often become confused as to which was when, and what came first. Santino feels that particular components of Halloween, Christmas, and St. Brigit's Day mumming have overlapped. Tad Teleja in his essay on trick-or-treating[5] asserts that today's colorful begging practice has three roots: the All Souls' Day tradition known as soul caking, the masked begging of Guy Fawkes Day, and peasant collections taken up for Saint Columba.

According to Teleja, the County Cork of Ireland enjoyed a mummers procession to mark All Hallows complete with young men, self-proclaimed ambassadors of Muck Olla (a boar known in Irish folk tales, not a God) lead by a young man wearing white robes and a horse's head (Lair Bhan, or white mare). His cohorts would parade noisily behind, blowing cow horns and in general raising the volume level as much as possible.[6]

In Scotland during the sixteenth century, young men would cook up amazing disguises with horrific masks, flitting from house to house and shop to shop, carrying turnip lanterns or kail-runt torches, singing their favorite rhymes and begging for apples, nuts, and copper coins. These packs of rowdy adolescents were called guisers, and this practice of guising lasted well into the twentieth century.[7]

In medieval Europe on All Souls' Day, beggars sought alms as payment for prayers they promised to say for the dead loved ones of those who gave them money. By eating a soul cake, the beggar or other individual would help to release someone from the torments of Purgatory.

Finally, in commemoration of Guy Fawkes' abortive attempt to blow up the Houses of Parliament in November of 1605, English children built bonfires, dressed rag effigies (the possible forerunner of the scarecrow) as "Guys," and begged money from strangers to purchase sweets and fireworks. Any one of these examples, including several I haven't cited, may have led to our European roots of the American ritual of trick-or-treating.

The point of all this noise, costuming, and begging folds neatly into a single theme—the creation of prosperity. Whether we take the Christian view of give unto others, or the Pagan ideology of every action has an equal reaction, we are still talking about each individual's general prosperity and the desire to allow that prosperity to grow by sharing with our fellow human. Therefore, in actuality, the practice of trick-or-treating is one of a focused magickal act. (Don't raise your eyebrows.) As you extend the prosperity to others, you are rewarded in kind.

Moving on to American tradition, we discover that modern Americans, in their search to counteract the consequences of Mischief Night, sought to eliminate vandalism by reinstituting the old European customs of house-begging and parades. We also find an early nineteenth century custom in New York City where children dressed in costume begged for pennies on Thanksgiving Day (as our traditional Thanksgiving was related to the original Halloween celebration). Regardless of the type of costume, these children were called Ragamuffins, and the custom remained alive in America until the 1930s, when the begging was switched from Thanksgiving to Halloween.[8]

From 1930 until 1970, the American trick-or-treating custom created a bonding between children and adult neighbors, and allowed the adults to control the mischief through the delights of promised goodies. From 1930 through 1960, children were almost always invited into the neighbor's home, and several magazines printed for the women of those generations indicated the proper way to prepare treats and handle their bizarre little visitors in correct, social decorum. Part of the fun for adults and children centered on guessing whose little face peered from behind the costumed one. Where cider and doughnuts were the prize of the 1930s, store-bought candies took precedence in the 1970s.

By 1970, most neighbors no longer allowed the children into their homes. The front porch became the limited shared environment, breaking down the bonding process, showing our growing surge toward isolation and anonymity—leading to a silent message of ultimate mistrust. During this time period, only teachers at school with class-driven Halloween parties kept up the tradition of the guessing game, offering a small prize to the child that could mask both their personality and their physical appearance. By the 1990s, most teachers no longer participated in this game.

As we near the millennium, sociologists and psychologists alike are worried that our children may be learning a negative economic lesson in the wake of bogus urban legends that have sprung up around our beloved practice of trick-or-treating. They fear that corporate America is teaching children to trust only store-bought products by established companies, delegitimizing homemade treats and, in turn, breeding continued mistrust between generations. Halloween is not their only concern. The attempt to sanitize our society by continuing to create nonessential rules could backfire, mushrooming into calamities that we never thought possible a century ago.[9]

Each year in my little town fewer lights illuminate the customary "front porch offering." Some of my neighbors claim that the holiday is just too expensive, others rattle on about the bogus Satan connection, and I think to myself, "Who are you to ruin a special day for children with such excuses?" No matter how tough life was for our family, my ancestors included, we always found within our hearts the room to give to the children. This year when the kids knock at your door (and you will answer, won't you?), remember that as you hand over your special contribution to those colorful little munchkins you are in actuality practicing a bit of magick thousands of years old. You are giving unto others. And, if it makes you feel better, ask them to sing a rhyme to you. I assure you that laughter will carry the day.

Bonfires, Fireworks, and Halloween Processions

As we've seen, processions on Samhain/Halloween from Paleopagan times until the present have been part of the norm. We've also discovered that humans love to have parades for all sorts of things, from sporting and political events to religious functions. Why do people get in a line (or some semblance of one) and march anywhere? Why do they dance in the streets? What is the purpose? We find the answer in the psychology of the group mind.

I never understood the emotional concept of the bonfire or the procession until I experienced them for myself on two separate occasions. Oh yes, I'd seen bonfires and been in a parade or two, but never one fashioned after our Paleopagan forebears. On the first occasion, I watched a Paleopagan reenactment complete with torches, costumed participants, drumming, and ritual dancing. With my mouth literally hanging open, I watched the dancers tease the cold wood with the torches, and I remember my awe as the flaming sticks ignited the wood in one fluid motion, sending a magnificent beast of sparks and fire roaring and clawing into the midnight sky. It was, to put it bluntly, a psychological rush.

On the second occasion, I had to leave a bonfire early. The path from this bonfire was long and winding, curling around the lip of a lake. Halfway back I happened to turn and look across the still, black water. I felt as if I'd been transported through time. Amazing. From a distance I watched the costumed dancers flit around the fire in a luminous oval, the sweat of their bodies glistening from heat and exhaustion. The drums rumbled, their Pagan beat echoing against the trees, lifting in a steady pulse to the star-knitted heavens. Occasionally a shout or peal of laughter bounced across the lake, the placid water catching the reflection of the flames. At that moment I knew exactly what the energy and emotion felt like around those ancient ritual fires. As a primal scream from one of those dancers struck my ears, I knew, too, the fear that the pious Christians must have felt as their eyes looked on such a strange scene, and the gut-craving reaction they experienced at the wild unknown of human abandonment. I wanted to go back, back into that cluster of stomping feet and wild revelry. I understood, too, why many people attend Native American powwows. There is an emotional bonding between the earth, the human, and the festivities, even if this bonding only lasts for a short time.

In European history, rhyming would take place during the hours of darkness, but during the hours of light children and young adults were busily searching for the right materials for the home or community bonfire.

While the term Bonfire Night once referred to Halloween, Northern Ireland has moved it and created a national holiday that celebrates the victory of the Protestant William III over the Catholic James II at the Battle of the Boyne. In Britain, Bonfire Night refers to November 5, Guy Fawkes Night, commemorating the apprehension and subsequent execution of the men who attempted to blow up Parliament in 1605. Regardless, the ancient roots of the Samhain bonfire traveled through various cultures and landed in the amalgam of American tradition, where revelers watched the flames and shot their guns (according to my grandfather) in a Pennsylvania farming town in 1905.

Although not an American tradition, fireworks were very much a part of Irish Halloween celebrations until the early 1970s, when the fireworks were banned due to the acceleration of terrorist activities. Up until that point, posters, cards, and other Halloween paraphernalia combined pictures of the traditional icons of ghosts and black cats with the colorful symbolism of fireworks.

Various historical records tell us of Halloween parades and processions throughout Europe beyond the Dark Ages, showing us that the Halloween parade survived, regardless of the hard-hitting practice of church officials and petty landowners. The *Dundee Advertiser* in 1871 reported on the Scottish festival held on Halloween at Balmoral Castle, known as "The Queen's Halloween":

. . . the people, both on the Balmoral and Abergeldie estates, turned out on Tuesday night, and formed a torchlight procession, which had a picturesque and imposing appearance. There were altogether from 180 to 200 torch-bearers; and her Majesty, with several members of the Royal family, viewed the scene with evident pleasure and satisfaction. Her Majesty remained for fully an hour an interested spectator of the proceedings. After the torch-bearers had promenaded for some time, the torches were heaped in a pile on the roadway a little to the west, and in full view from the windows of the Castle. Empty boxes and other materials were soon added and in a short time a splendid bonfire blazed famously, a gentle breeze helping to fan the flames.

Her Majesty, the Prince and Princess Louise, the Princess Beatrice and the ladies and gentlemen of the suite, then retired indoors, and took up positions at the windows to see the rest of the merry-making. Dancing was begun with great vigour round the bonfire. The demonstration culminated in a vehicle containing a well got-up effigy of the Halloween woman being drawn to the fire by a band of sturdy Highlanders. The effigy had a number of boys for a guard of honour, headed by the piper, and in the rear came her Majesty's yager, whose workmanship the effigy was. The fire was kept up for a long time with fresh fuel, and when all had danced till they could almost dance no longer, the health of her Majesty was proposed by the yager, and responded to with the utmost enthusiasm, accompanied by three times three rounds of vociferous cheering. The festivities ended with a ball in the castle sponsored by the Queen.[10]

One of the grandest American Halloween masquerades occurs in the New York City Greenwich Village Halloween parade, where hundreds of thousands of people gather on New York's Seventh Avenue at dusk to watch the stream of Pagan icons meander through the Village. Unlike more sophisticated community parades, there are no sponsors, no prizes, no grandstands, or local merchant vendor opportunities, yet, to the Big Apple residents, the celebration remains a constant delight. The parade began in the early 1970s as an exhibition of theater artist Ralph Lee's grotesque masks. Although Lee reportedly lost interest in the parade when it grew so large that no one noticed his masks anymore, it continues to attract approximately 100,000 marchers and 250,000 spectators annually. The Village Halloween Parade is different from other community processions because it makes no claim to respectability, virtue, or ethnic compartmentalism. It is, in a word, just plain fun.

Masks and Costumes

Scholars are currently tussling over the origin of masks and costumes. Some feel that these fun forays into fantasy were worn to scare off things that screech in the night, where others are firmly entrenched in the ideology that costumes and masks brought the individual wearer closer to the spirit realms by creating a sympathetic energy between themselves and the natural world. Regardless of the reasoning, costumes and masks pop up frequently when studying the roots and growth of Halloween. Today, parents and children alike vie for the right to parade around town, dressed in their favorite fantasy finery. (In the sixties our parents only did that behind closed doors at the neighbor's Halloween party, unless, of course, there was a parade nearby that you could use as an excuse.) Today, in Dillsburg, Pennsylvania, moms work months before the Harvest Parade to concoct magnificent costumes for the kiddies (and themselves), while dads work diligently in their garages trying to come up with the miniature float that will win the grand prize. National Theme Productions, a costume rental agency, reports that in 1980, one in every four adults aged eighteen to forty wore a costume and that sixty percent of their rentals were adult oriented. Price does not seem to be a problem as we circle the millennium, and adults are willing to pay over $150 for rentals or costume purchases related to the holiday, let alone the cash used for cards, food, and decorations.

Wearing masks and costumes has traveled from Celtic mythos into present-day Halloween practices in America and the Day of the Dead practices in Mexico and South America. Like house-begging, the religious impact that originally created these customs has taken a back seat in the modern American holiday, almost to the point of total anonymity. To the modern American, Halloween has become a holiday to role play in their favorite disguise and become whomever they desire. Its only rivalry is in boxed role-playing games and an even bigger competition, the Internet, where every day can provide a psychological escape in mental costuming. But neither of these has the hands-on creativity and the competition we experience when designing the best Halloween costume ever.

Today's Halloween costumes fulfill the human need to live out a fantasy where there are no consequences. Dr. Steven Alter, a practicing clinical psychologist and an Adelphi University psychology professor, states that "wearing a mask allows us to experience another aspect of our identity without shaking the true identity that we normally use." This may indicate why Halloween costumes have become so enticing to American adults.

Were masks originally created by Paleopagans and the early Celtic peoples to entice the good spirits or to scare away the bad ones? No one really knows. We have no concrete evidence either way, but we do have mountains of supposition from religious and scientific camps covering the past 2,000 years. What is evident is that the practice of using masks and unusual dress reflects the socialization of any era. From the hobo, the Witch, or the fairy princess in the 1930s to Darth Vader, Power Rangers, and Mutant Ninja Turtles in the 1990s, chosen costumes show the icons of the decade and the need for fantasy as well as provide a record for future historians. Recent studies of American corporate structures show that allowing workers to wear costumes and compete for prizes actually enhances the image of the company, raises morale, and humanizes their public presentation to customers.[11]

The Southern Influence on Halloween

The inhabitants of the southern states in America have added to the compendium of Halloween lore. African slaves whispered their magickal secrets in the kitchens of plantation owners, and the wives of the owners whispered their own European lore back. With the added influence of the French, Cuban, and Haitian emigrants into the southern states and the mixing of their individual lore and traditions, new practices exploded into a cauldron of myth and mysticism.

> Like the volatile mix of pagan and Catholic influences that created much of the European Halloween lore, the combination of Voudoun and Catholicism in parts of the South produced a folklore just as full of eerie ritual, magick and the supernatural. Marie Laveau for example—the 19th century high priestess of Voudoun—was famous for feats of magick that incorporated potent symbols of each religion. . . . Over the course of the nineteenth century, some Voudoun beliefs were assimilated into the European folklore, producing an especially spicy Halloween mythology in terms of spirits, divination and witchcraft.[12]

The practice of cooking an entire dinner backwards on Halloween Eve originated from the southern states. Young women hoped that by doing this process they could see the face of their future husband at the end of the meal.

Switching Holidays

There are some European customs that found their place not at their Halloween point of origin but instead settled in American New Year celebrations. For example, bell ringing, prevalent in Europe on All Hallows Eve, was outlawed by King Henry VIII and didn't make it across the waters of the Atlantic for Halloween, but did resurface on the American New Year's Eve. It appears that when Henry finally bit the dust, the bell ringing tradition began again but was ousted by Queen Elizabeth because she did not like the "superfluous ringing of the bells on All Hallows Eve"[13] that she felt was a Catholic practice. Likewise, the tradition of a group of people staying together until after midnight for ensuring prosperity and protection in the coming year also moved to the American New Year's Eve, though I doubt anyone participating in this celebration has a clue as to how this practice first began. We can trace the American custom of leaving "goodies" for Santa Claus and his reindeer from the Celts and Romans, who left bowls of bread and milk by the hearth to feed the spirits of the departed, or to appease the sidhe (faeries).

Now let's take a look at some of your favorite Halloween symbols and superstitions. You might be surprised at their origins!

Notes

1. W. C. Hazlitt, *Dictionary of Faiths & Folklore Beliefs, Superstitions and Popular Customs*, Reeves and Turner, 1905, page 299.

2. Jack is "a hideous little being somewhat human in form, though covered with hair like a dog. It had great goggle eyes, and thick sausage-like lips that opened from ear to ear. In height it seldom exceeded four or five feet, and was quite slender in form, but such was its power of locomotion that none on the swiftest horse could overtake it or even escape from it." William Owens, "Folklore of the Southern Negroes," *The Negro and his Folklore in Nineteenth Century Periodicals*, ed. Bruce Jackson, Austin University of Texas Press, 1967, pages 146-47.

3. John Santino, *The Hallowed Eve, Dimensions of Culture in a Calendar Festival in Northern Ireland*, The University Press of Kentucky, 1998.

4. In Britain, beggars sought alms as payment for prayers that they promised to say for the dead loved ones of the charitable individual. By eating a soul cake, the beggar or other individual would help to release someone from Purgatory. There is a conflict as to whether Purgatory is a place where one is tormented or a place where one waits a particular period of time before one can enter heaven, depending upon your religious views.

5. Tad Tuleja, "Trick or Treat—PreTexts and Contexts," in *Halloween and Other Festivals of Life and Death*, edited by Jack Santino, University of Tennessee Press, 1994.

6. Lesley Pratt Bannatyne, *Halloween: An American Holiday, An American History*, Facts on File, Inc., page 67.

7. F. Marian McNeill, *Halloween: Its Origins, Rites and Ceremonies in Scottish Tradition*, Albyn Press, 1970, pages 30-31.

8. Bannatyne, page 67.

9. Joel Best and Horiuchi, "The Razor Blade in the Apple: The Social Construction of Urban Legends," Social Problems, Volume 32, No. 5, June 1985, page 497.

10. Hazlitt, page 299.

11. From "Carnival, Control, and Corporate Culture in Contemporary Halloween Celebrations" by Russell W. Belk, Professor of Business Administration at the University of Utah. His research primarily involves the meanings of possessions and materialism. Also, *Halloween and Other Festivals of Death and Life*, edited by Jack Santino, University of Tennessee, 1994.

12. Bannatyne, page 86.

13. Hazlitt, page 299.

chapter

3

HALLOWEEN SYMBOLS AND SUPERSTITIONS

On Hallowe'en the thing
you must do
Is pretend that nothing
can frighten you
An' if somethin' scares you
and you want to run
Jus' let on like
it's Hallowe'en fun.

—FROM AN EARLY NINETEENTH-CENTURY
HALLOWEEN POSTCARD

53

Autumn breezes swish chilly skirts, sending colorful leaves scurrying across sidewalks and streets. In rural areas, wood fires tickle the nose and smudge the horizon with velvety smoke. Farmers haul out flatbed trailers loaded with pumpkins and gourds, ready to help youngsters pick the right size and shape for that memorable jack-o'-lantern. Local preserves, fresh-baked pies, and bushels of apples barrel through the supermarket checkout at dizzying speed. By October 1, the stores pack their aisles with colorful costumes, masks, and the "must have" paraphernalia for this year's trick-or-treaters. Crafty mothers and grandmothers search the fabric stores for patterns and material to make that best costume ever while children eagerly rattle "I wanna be . . . ," which changes every thirty seconds.

The blood quickens as the sounds, smells, and sights of Halloween overtake our senses, propelling us into that special time of year where scary stuff is presented to delight and enchant us. What are the traditional symbols of Halloween, and where did they come from? Often created or fueled by historical inaccuracies, most of the Halloween symbols we use today find their roots in the superstitions of the European peoples.

Black Cats

Our modern Halloween just wouldn't be the same without the traditional pictures of the black cat— claws extended, back arched, and tail fluffed! How did our favorite kitties wander into Halloween? We first find cat mythology in ancient goddess worship; the Teutonic Freya rode in a chariot drawn by cats, Artemis–Diana often appeared in cat form and, of course, we have the Egyptian deity Bast. Domestic cats were not introduced into Northern Europe until after 1,050 C.E., and the wild cat in Scotland sometimes cited by historians appears to be a wild hare. Again, a language conversion might be responsible for this error.

White hares were thought to be sacred by the ancient Celts, and they believed that these animals could contain the souls of the dead who wished to visit the living. This does not mean they thought the rabbits were the dead, but that the rabbit could be a vessel for a temporary and welcomed visitation. There is no evidence that the Celts believed in reincarnation or in permanent transmigration of the soul.

Checking history, we find only one fully developed centralized religion that honored our feline friends. During the cat's two-thousand-year incarnation in Egyptian history, the cat came to symbolize the goddess energy of the religion.[1] The earliest known portrait of Bast was found in a temple of the fifth dynasty (about 3,000 B.C.E.). When the people wanted a fierce goddess to protect them, they called on Sekhmet; when they wanted a gentler goddess, or more personal assistance, they called upon Bast. The Egyptian trinity was known as Sekhmet-Bast-Ra.

The negative superstition tied to cats could have begun with the Romans when a foolish Roman soldier killed a cat and a mob broke into his house and removed him from this earthly plane. Several centuries later, the negative association with cats came from Inquisitor Nicholas Remy, who claimed that all cats were demons. In 1387, Lombard Witches were said to worship the devil as a cat and medieval Christians exposed cats to torture and fire along with Witches. At certain festivals, such as Midsummer, Easter, and Shrove Tuesday, it was customary to burn cats in wicker cages in accordance with these church beliefs. The cats, however, appear to have gotten their revenge as the Black Death, a form of bubonic plague, killed over twenty-seven million people during the Middle Ages. Had the church let the people keep their cats, the fleas (which carry the disease) on the rats may not have brought Europe to its knees.

The cat, with its association to goddess worship, was not a favorite of the Christian Church. As the church had already devalued women, subjecting human females to torture and murder, what was a mere cat? Once the early Christians got it into their heads that Witches could change themselves into cats, there was no stopping them. Trial after trial, women were tortured into babbling that they had turned themselves into these sleek and sneaky animals. The myth gained momentum and has continued to live in horror films of today.

As superstition in America began to abate in the 1930s and 40s, the black cat became a fun and familiar symbol of Halloween. Already linked for centuries to

Witches, these furry friends vaulted into the limelight of Halloween parties without any difficulty at all. Once seen as unlucky visitors in any household, the modern Halloween feline does his or her duty by scaring away the nasties that go bump in the night. Cats, however, like to show off their catches to their human mommies and daddies, so you might not want to open the door to see kitty's surprise on All Hallow's Eve![2]

The Pitchfork

Most modern Americans link the pitchfork with the devil, and what devil costume at Halloween would be complete without one? But, truth be told, the idea of the pitchfork originally had nothing to do with Satan and his minions.

Various cultures, including the Celts, used the trident as a male fertility symbol. In India, the trident bearer was the bridegroom of Kali. Other Pagan gods, such as Neptune and Poseidon, carried a trident as the symbol of fertility associated with the birth waters of the sea. The association with the trident and the devil begins with the early Christian Church, which tried to squelch the idea of fertility (it might be fun) and handed the symbol over to their devil (as he was known for sexual depravity) because of its association with Celtic fertility imagery. Celtic myth indicated that the trident was the key to the Holy Door. As the trident was generally recognized as male equipment in Pagan tradition, Renaissance devils were often painted with forked body parts.

Despite the church's objections, the pitchfork continued as the focus of harvest festivals (it was a useful tool) decorated with flowers, leaves, vines, sheaves of dried corn, and ribbons. Today, if you want to find a real pitchfork, you'll probably have to go to a farm museum or dig around in someone's basement or barn. They are, after all, dangerous because they have pointy metal things on them. My great-grandfather Baker (of German descent) had a pitchfork made for the Dillsburg Harvest Festival. He painted it gold and family history indicates that he led the Harvest Fair parade with this fertility symbol, marching along with a magnificent grin on his face. If the people of the town knew what he was doing, they would probably have experienced heart failure.

Scarecrows, Corn Dollies, and Snigging the Cailleach

Ask any farmer and you'll learn that scarecrows don't really scare birds; in fact, they make a mighty handy perch. The scarecrow is quite a magickal fellow, who for centuries has been guarding the fields of humankind not from our feathered friends, but from a menace far more powerful and all-encompassing—crop failure. (Well, my dad might pick a fight on this one because the birds just love his sweet pea vines . . .) As ghoulish as it may sound, the original scarecrow appears to have been a real person who was sacrificed on ancient fields to feed the land and encourage bountiful crops, though historical records indicate this practice most likely occurred in the spring, at the time of planting.[3]

In Finland the scarecrow is known as Pellon Pekko, meaning "Little Peter of the Field." His job is to protect and fertilize the crops.[4] The burning of effigies is also an old practice, used for a variety of purposes, including religious and political, and practiced all over the world for centuries. The scarecrow symbology may have crept into current Halloween practices through one of three avenues: The rhymers/mummers of Europe; the practice of burning the wicker man (Druid); or the effigy burnings celebrated on Guy Fawkes Day in Britain.

The corn dolly is entirely different. This European practice centers on making a doll out of the last stalk of corn harvested in the fall, although other plants from the fields such as barley, oats, wheat, or rye could be used. To the early Pagans she was the embodiment of the harvest, and they thought of quite a few interesting magickal things to do with her. Some poured water over the doll as a fertility charm; or she might be wed to a corn man, attend the harvest festival dance, be fed to farm animals to protect their health, or be burned in the community bonfire as an offering of thanks. In our home the corn dolly is "put to bed" until spring, where she is reawakened and plowed into the new garden.

The corn dolly has an association with a practice in Ireland called "snigging the Cailleach," though upon research, we find the Cailleach Bera (Calilleach Beara, Cailleac Bhearra) in Irish legend and the Cailleach Bheur in the lore of the Scottish Highlands. With the harvesting of the last field, the final, large swathe or "sward" of corn was taken and plaited by fours, then tied and taken to the house where the harvest feast would be held. The homeowner and his wife both wore the plait for a few minutes, giving thanks for this year's harvest and prayers for the next. In some homes the plait would be used as a table centerpiece and in others it was hung on the wall above the master of the house. Brightly colored ribbons might be added to the braid to brighten this festive occasion. When the feasting and dancing were finished, the plait was hung from a rafter in the kitchen to further the prosperity of the homestead. According to one Irish account, the Cailleach was supposed to be a wee, small woman wearing a red or green cloak.[5] The word "Cailleach" means Old Woman, and it is possibly from here that we derive the Witch seen as an old hag. Indeed, nicknames for the Cailleach were "hag" and "old hag." The Cailleach Bera is a Celtic corn spirit in Irish folklore, but she is also a strong, supernatural being of immense cunning, her skin of yellow hue. Some say that she carried an apron full of stones, challenging those who wished to harvest the fields, and could turn into a hare to race upon the fields.[6] Her mythos stems from the Beare peninsula in west Cork in the province of Munster, Ireland.

In Scotland this powerful lady is described with a hideous blue face, wearing plaid and carrying a staff, walking stick, or mallet. She ushers in winter by washing her plaid in the whirlpool of Corryvreckan. When she is done, the plaid of Scotland is virgin white.[7] Here, she is a guardian of wild animals (deer, boar, goats, cattle, and wolves). She also guards the streams and wells and is considered the personification of winter from Samhain to Beltainne. If you make her mad she will unleash the Faoiltach (wolf storm) to prevent the Beltainne warmth from returning to the land. She is responsible for changing the landscape. Whether we look at the Irish or Scottish version of this venerable lady, she stands for the common sense, intelligence, diplomacy, and prudence that we earn as we face our golden years of life.

Some modern-day Witches are insulted when they see the hag flying across front doors, in newspaper articles, or dancing over the Internet. This year, when you look at our beloved hag, think of wisdom and the history our strong Cailleach carries with her into the millennium.

Skeletons and the Mexican Day of the Dead

I know'd it, know'd it
Indeed I know'd it brother
I know'd it—Weeeeee!
Dem bones gonna rise again.

—Anonymous Early American Ballad

We can't have Halloween without jiggling bones and skeletal leers. The fascination with skeletons dates back to the Paleopagans and later European mythos, where many tribal peoples preserved the heads or skulls of their ancestors, which were painted, dressed, and displayed in prominent positions at clan gatherings, or were consulted as oracles with appropriate offerings. The doctrine of the church forbade the burial of a headless body (thank goodness!) and the custom eventually passed from practice, though in European households, shrines to the dead continued in use.

It is likely that our fascination with skeletons in our modern American Halloween celebrations has a strong link with El Dia de los Muertos—the Day of the Dead—and the tossing of Mexican culture into the melting pot of America. This delightful celebration begins on the eve of October 31. Often called Los Dias de los Muertos (because more than one day is involved, depending on the local celebration), it is considered by many Mexicans to be their most important festival. Some scholars believe that the Mexican holiday is a conglomeration of Celtic, Catholic, and Aztec mythos and, when you look at the festival as a whole, you can see where that determination came from with the history given in chapter 1. The Day of the Dead includes the belief held by the Aztecs that the souls of the dead returned to Mexico with the migration of the monarch butterfly each fall.

The word "somber" does not figure into this Mexican celebration, as this is a time of parades, brilliant costumes, feasting, and the act of honoring the dead with love. The townspeople dress as skeletons, mummies, ghosts, and ghouls, parading through town carrying an open coffin complete with a live passenger dressed as a corpse. Skeletons and skulls abound, made from chocolate, bread, molded sugar, and assorted candies. Handmade puppets, called *calacas*, add to the fun and frivolity. Each family sets up an altar in their home to honor those who have passed away in their family (or close friends). On November 1, family members go to the gravesite of their loved one and perform required maintenance such as weeding and raking. Some families go at night on October 31 with picnic baskets, candles, and musical instruments to serenade the dead, remaining there until dawn breaks over the horizon.

In Texas, traditional names for the holiday reflect the difference between the Mexican holiday and the Tex-Mex holiday. In Texas the day is called El Dia de los Difuntos (the Day of the Deceased) or El Dia de los Finados (the Day of the Finished and/or Departed). The Tex-Mex remembrance of the dead acknowledges the importance of the deceased's separation from this world. Celebrations symbolically affirm this separation while acknowledging reconnection with the loved one through memory. Here we find both a community celebration and a religious practice. For many communities, this day serves as a social gathering. Memories of the dead are often framed by graveside encounters between old friends and relatives, family stories, and limited feasting (as food is not the central element of these get-togethers).

In Texas, the central meeting for the family is All Souls' Day, and in Mexico the focus of the holiday is around a special altar in the home, church, or sometimes the cemetery, where flowers, candles, incense, and offerings of favorite foods are placed. The altar is the power point, a door between the living and the dead. It is believed that those items on the altar will attract and soothe the departed spirit. In Texas, many families prefer to perform grave maintenance at this time, then add handcrafted items, fresh flowers, wreaths and, due to increasing inflation, mass-produced materials such as pumpkins, black balloons, paper ghosts, and other images of the holiday. According to Mary J. Andrade, researcher and author of "Through the Eyes of the Soul: Day of the Dead in Mexico," special foods prepared as offerings to be placed on the altars are called *ofrendas*, meaning mortuary food.

It is through the Spanish-Catholic folk customs of the Day of the Dead that we can best see the original European Celtic festival and early Christian practices surrounding Hallowmas and All Souls' Eve. Rather than destroy the custom, as the American Puritans tried to do, the Mexican and South American peoples pulled this early Celtic holiday into their local customs and expanded on the celebration.

Posttraumatic Puritan syndrome keeps many Americans from fully enjoying the idea of happy dead or dancing down to the bones. Don't let this awful psychological condition keep you from enjoying the delightful, whirling skeletons![8]

Ghosts and Haints

Every culture contains its share of ghost stories, whether we are talking 2,000 years ago or last winter. The words "guest" and "ghost" find their roots in the Germanic "geist," which originally meant a spirit of a dead ancestor invited to tribal celebrations such as Samhain and other solemn events. This sort of ghost manifested as a benevolent spirit among the living.

The Paleopagan belief that the human souls trapped in the bodies of animals could be released on Samhain and allowed to enter their new human incarnations gave rise to the early Christian idea that the dead could inhabit animals, therefore the animals became bewitched and rabid. From animals, the idea jumped to the possession of humans as well. Twisted by the early Christians, this simple belief became part of the "possession" syndrome used to gain power for the church through stories of fear.

Today, unfortunate accidents, suicides, wrongful deaths, and murders keep the human imagination alive with tortured spirits waiting to capture the attention of the unsuspecting living. Unrequited passion or the loss of a loved one through disease or natural means urges the psyche to believe that those departed have not abandoned the living. Oral legends, books, movies, and religion help to fan the flames of the promise of an afterlife. After all, no one wants to believe that this is all there is. And if there is an afterlife, then naturally those who you have loved will want to visit you, right?

Technically speaking, a ghost represents a human (or animal) that has physically passed from the earth plane, yet his or her spirit either comes to visit on occasion or remains behind, stuck between this world and the hereafter. A haint is negative energy expelled by a living individual(s) that coalesces as a mass of energy. Where we assume that ghosts have the capacity to think, haints do not have this luxury. You will find haints in negative environments or places of great emotional distress, such as hospitals, prisons, bars, and drug hangouts. Haints are not confined to buildings; they can also be found in the woods, the deserts, or at the sea shore, and are drawn to violence, from which they feed. In most circumstances, ghosts motor about on their own steam, sticking close to loved ones or physical items that meant a lot to them in life. It is difficult for most humans to discern between the activities of a ghost or a haint.

Poltergeist activity (for the record) is most often found in homes with teens, mentally challenged, or physically violent personalities. Many scientists believe that poltergeists represent energy that has coalesced, like a haint, and prowls the home of the person it belongs to, meting out justice to whomever has mistreated or been unfair to the owner of the energy.

As Samhain was associated with the dead and a belief in a land where the dead stay forever young, it is natural for our American Halloween to carry vestiges of haunted tales, ghosts, and vaporous things that flit about, merry and menacing. After all, the early Christians replaced the Celtic mythos with a place called heaven, therefore affirming an afterlife of some sort, so it is not surprising that the belief in ghosts persists.

While older Americans enjoy a frightfully haunting tale, parents have also created the "friendly" ghost for the little ones, who fits in quite well with the modern Halloween and actually returns the holiday to its original intentions where visitors of the other world are concerned. The Catholic ritual of offering prayers for the dead remains a firm holdover from the Celtic practices. Modern Witches, Druids, and other magickal individuals also offer prayers to the dead on Halloween and often participate in Dumb Suppers (see page 172) in honor of those family members or close friends who have passed away—again, a direct link to our Pagan past.

Next time the lights go out on Halloween, or you hear footsteps on the stair, or a knocking at the door, it just may be someone you loved who has stopped by to pay you a friendly visit. Legend says that this is the time when the veil between the worlds is the thinnest . . . and we all know that within every legend there lies a kernel of truth.

Witches

Today, there are approximately 1.2 million practicing Witches (Wiccans) in the United States—about the same collective number as writers or firefighters (just to give you an idea). WitchCraft is the fastest growing religion in the United States, particularly among white middle-class Americans, although individuals of various nationalities, cultures, and races all practice it. Although you might assume that teenagers are responsible for the highest number of Crafters, this is not the case. Most individuals convert between the ages of twenty-one and forty-five, and there is a growing number of individuals who are assimilating Craft practices into an already established religious pattern of their choice.

Illogically, the early Christians preached that Witches could provide themselves with all the wealth anyone could want, yet the church left the rich alone and went straight for the poor or outcast individual. Accusations were fueled by petty spite, village feuds, the need for dominance, or the lust for money. Witches were convenient scapegoats for doctors who failed to cure their patients. Most persecutions found their root in superstition, narrowness of mind, and jealousy assisted by cruel and vicious laws. And pity the woman who voiced her dissent in matters of church politics and had red or gray hair or blue, gray, or green eyes![9]

Let us keep in mind, however, that up until the 1300s, the services of Witches as healers and diviners of the future were used by the church and noblemen alike.[10]

How many individuals were murdered due to the European Witch craze? Adding the reported numbers from Scotland, Spain, England, Belgium, France, Finland, Switzerland, and southwest Germany, and taking the percentages from the years 1563–1727,[11] we come up with the following reported figures: 1,869 men; 6,122 women; total reported executions: 7,491, of which eighty-two percent were female. Please note that these numbers do not report previous executions (1300–1562) nor are they the total number of executions during those years due to the loss of records, nonreported cases, and unreported areas.

In its desire to devalue women, the familiar Witch-Hag whom we associate today with our modern Halloween rose to the surface of the medieval Christian mind. Several Pagan goddesses are depicted as older women, in celebration of the elderly, such as Hecate, the Cailleach, and the Crone aspect of the female trinity of Maiden, Mother, and Crone. The church needed to denigrate the elderly woman and remove her authority from society, therefore she was vilified. Many elderly women were tortured, burned, or hanged simply because of their age.

Today, just about every little girl in our society, at one time or another, has chosen to costume herself as a Witch, though her taste might run from the pretty Witch to the bizarre creature with the wart on her nose. The pointed Witches' hat actually symbolizes the cone of power, which is the energy a magickal person raises to assist him or herself in prayer, and the broom corresponds to fertility rites practiced by European peasants to ensure the growth of crops.

If you choose a Witch's costume this Halloween, remember the sobering history of what you are portraying—the thousands of innocent women and children (and a few men, too) who were sacrificed because of their religious or cultural preferences (or worse, just because they were different). Hold your head up and wear your Witch's garb proudly in their honor.

Vampires and Bats

There's nothing like a good bite right before begging for candy, and our friend the vampire can certainly provide this little service for us. The legend of the vampire found its lasting existence fueled by superstition surrounding historical acts of cruelty by select European leaders and peasant fears, including the horrendous historical character Vlad the Impaler.

The legend of the vampire appears to be a amalgam of various superstitions that rolled into one entity: (1) The widespread belief that the dead could return to visit the living through Samhain, Halloween, or All Saints' Day; (2) The existence of real maniacs running around and hurting people and allowing a superstition to cover their evil tracks; (3) Premature burial, which often occurred before embalming became a necessary practice; (4) Gossip—a person who was an outcast when alive remained outcast after death; and (5) Plagues and epidemics. [12]

Ever since Homer's time, western nations had the fixed idea that blood combined with the light of the moon could recall the dead to life, at least temporarily.[13] Churchmen of the Middle Ages claimed that a woman who exposed her body to the moonlight would conceive and bear a vampire child. The church sanctioned the belief in vampires and taught that vampires could only walk under the light of the moon. Their prime concern? Finding blood.

We find the belief in vampires appearing in Babylon and Assyria, where it was thought that the dead could rise and walk the earth, seeking sustenance from the living. The vampires of Crete, called Katalkanas, were blamed for ill deeds, and were said to live in the mountains. In Germany, food was buried with the dead, or rice and grain scattered on the grave, to assuage the hunger pangs of the Nachzehrer, who might issue forth from the grave in the form of a pig. In Bulgaria, the Vrykolaka were said to be passive vampires in life who became active after death. Up until the twentieth century, vampire depictions contained horrendous faces, malformed body parts, little hair, and drooling spittle—sometimes appearing more as an ugly beast on two feet rather than carrying pleasant, human attributes (until Anne Rice made them sexy!).

Today, the vampire fan club includes not only a real underground society but thousands of vampire enthusiasts enamored with the idea of a handsome cut of a man (or woman) quite capable of charming the blood right out of your pulsing veins. The more modern vampire tends to go in two directions—the "bad" vampire and the "good" vampire (where the good vampire finds true love in a human woman and kills only bad people). The association with the lifestyle of the vampire leads him (or her) to the logical link with Halloween—a night for the dead, undead (perhaps the correct term these days would be "living impaired"), and quaking living.

The vampire's association with Halloween is tenuous, as the vampire legend does not depend on or encompass this holiday, but if ghosts can walk this night, then why can't the vampires? Our association with the vampire, the bat, and the Witch come from two different sources. First, we all know that there is a type of vampire bat that drinks the blood of animals, which is therefore associated with the mythical vampire. Historical references link bats to Samhain bonfires, where the light of the fire drew moths, which in turn provided a feeding frenzy for bats. When the burning of the Witches commenced, the same principle applied—thus the superstitious believed that a Witch could turn herself into a bat, or that her spirit could fly away in the shape of a bat, because moths and bats were drawn to the burning Witches.

Today, every American Halloween party or parade would not be legitimate unless we have our swarm of little vampires, flashing their capes and baring their pointy fangs. Warning—just don't go out of the house on Halloween without that holy water or wooden stake!

Werewolves

Belief in the werewolf probably dates back to Paleopagan times, when the spirits of animals were both revered and feared. Further on in history, we discover that lycanthropy (werewolfism) finds its root name from Apollo Lycaeus (Wolfish Apollo), who was worshiped in the famous Lyceum or "Wolf temple" where Socrates taught. Apollo was mated to Artemis, known in some mythos as the divine Wolf Bitch. The She-Wolf was another aspect of the goddess trinity, and her legends move through various races and cultures. Significance here is placed on the belief that the goddess or god could shapeshift into an animal form. The werewolf legend of people turning into wolves (and back again) stems from this tribal belief.

Many myths, from Celtic Ireland through Germany, insist that if a person wears a wolf pelt, he or she can transform into the spirit beast. In Mercia during the tenth century A.D., there was a revival of Pagan learning under two Druidic priests, one of whom was named Werewolf. This name of "spirit-wolf" seems to have been applied to opponents of Christianity in general. About 1000 C.E., the word "werewolf" was taken to mean "outlaw"[14]—probably with its association to the renegade Druid priest. Criminals were hanged beside wolves, and the Saxon word for gallows means "wolf-tree."

Another story traceable to wolf-clan traditions, which may have its source in Germany, is the story of Little Red Riding Hood. The red garment and the offering of food to a "grandmother" in the deep woods (the grandmother wore a wolf skin) are symbolic of devouring and resurrection. It is thought that a woven red hood was the distinguishing mark of a prophetess or priestess. As death and resurrection are a large portion of the early Samhain beliefs, it is no wonder we find werewolves associated with the holiday of Halloween.

Medieval tales of numerous executions in France and Germany show that it was as dangerous to be a werewolf as it was to be a Witch. Historical records indicate the torture and murder of several men and women who were made to confess that they had acquired this shapeshifting ability, naturally through a pact with the Christian devil. It is possible that "serial killers" are not all that modern (skipping Jack the Ripper, of course), and that some of the earliest mass killers were considered vampires and werewolves, for killing without guilt is attributable to the animal condition, not the human one. We find the case of Peter Stubb, the infamous Werewolf of Cologne, accused of killing numerous women and children, to be one of the most frightening trials of an individual accused of actually being a werewolf. Two women, his daughter and his mistress, were sentenced as accomplices, and Peter Stubb met an incredibly horrendous death at the hands of his judges, while the women suffered the fate of burning at the stake.[15] Although this could be another urban legend gone wild—as with the Witch torture, hangings, and burnings mentioned earlier—this might be a case of a real medieval serial killer. France appears to have the worst case of werewolf mania, where many people were burned during the sixteenth century, including sufferers from porphyria (a genetic disease), rabies victims, ergot poisoning, and of course, the true criminal.[16]

Where wolves have resided, many tribes around the world have associated great power and mysticism to the animal and, in several cultures, the wolf was not seen as a "bad" beast. In reality, we know that the wolf is a highly social, intelligent, and friendly animal. The Celts were known to cross-breed wolves with hounds to produce a powerful dog for battle, and some Scotch traditions use the wolf as their totem (MacLennans and Mac Tyre).[17]

Whether you plan to walk on four paws or two this Halloween, take into consideration the original, honorable mythos of the werewolf, and act appropriately—though it's okay to howl at the moon, something all "good" werewolves are prone to do.

Or so they say . . .

Superstitions

In researching Halloween's history, we find a delightful compendium of superstitions associated either with the harvest season in general or with Halloween in particular. The word "superstition" means any or all of the following: an ignorant or irrational fear of what is unknown or mysterious, especially the fear of some invisible existence or existences, specifically, religious belief or practice (or both) founded on irrational fear or credulity; and excessive or unreasonable religious scruples produced by credulous fears.

- All souls in Purgatory are released for forty-eight hours from All Hallows Eve. On these nights they are free (Gaelic).

- On Halloween, the wind blowing over the feet of the deceased bears sighs to the houses of those about to die within the year (Wales).

- If you go to a crossroads at Halloween and listen to the wind, you will learn all the most important things that will befall you during the next twelve months.

- If you take a three-legged footstool and sit at a crossroads while the church clock is striking twelve on Halloween, you will hear proclaimed aloud the names of the church parishioners doomed to die within the next twelve months. If you throw an article of clothing belonging to any one of those doomed people into the air and call out their name, you can keep death from stalking at their door (Highlands of Scotland).

- To ensure fertility of crops during the coming year, make a circuit of the fields with a lighted torch on Halloween (England).

- On Halloween, force all the sheep and lambs to pass through a hoop of rowan wood to ward off Witches and faeries (Strathspey, England).

- A gambler who hides under the tendrils of the blackberry bush and invokes the aid of the ancients will always have good luck with the cards (Ireland).

- If you hear footsteps following you on Halloween, you should not look around, for it is the dead who are following, and if you meet their gaze, you will die (Ireland).

- On Halloween Eve, do not look at your shadow in the moonlight, or you shall be next to haunt a graveyard (England).

- Do not go hunting on Halloween Eve as you may wound a wandering spirit (England).

- Children born on Halloween will enjoy lifelong protection against evil spirits and will be endowed with the gift of second sight (rural America).

Summary

The ghosts of Halloween's past have not lain themselves to a peaceful rest. They dance and cavort through the collective unconscious of the people, and emerge each October 31 to once again remind us of our tribal roots, of fears we do not wish to face, and of the possibility of life after death. Through the symbols of Samhain—the bonfire, the masks, the scarecrow, and the beloved dead—and through the symbols of early Christian superstitions—the black cat, the vampire, the werewolf, the Witch burnings—we find the interesting kink of a holiday birthed from one religion and perverted by another. Modern Americans have seized Halloween with renewed vigor, spinning the symbolism into yet a new avenue of historical lore. What will Halloween be like in 2010? That's entirely up to you.

Notes

1. "The only fully-developed cult of the cat existed in Egypt and it lasted over two thousand years." Patricia Dale-Green, *Cult of the Cat,* Barre Publishing, 1963, page 1.

2. Veterinarians advise keeping some pets in a separate room when you have trick-or-treaters, and to never give pets leftover candy. They can get very sick. Also, don't put a heavy costume on your pet, it isn't good for them.

3. John Holland Smith, *The Death of Classical Paganism,* Scribner, 1976.

4. Barbara Walker, *The Woman's Encyclopedia of Myths and Secrets,* Harper Collins, 1983.

5. Jack Santino, *The Hallowed Eve—Dimensions of Culture in a Calendar Festival in Northern Ireland,* The University Press of Kentucky, 1998, page 77.

6. Carol Rose, *Spirits, Fairies, Leprechauns, and Goblins—An Encyclopedia,* W. W. Norton & Company, 1996, page 60.

7. Lynn Webster Wilde, *Celtic Women in Legend, Myth and History,* Cassell (distributed by Sterling), 1997.

8. For more information on the Day of the Dead, there is a fantastic website sponsored by the Chicano Library at UCLA: http://latino/sscnet/ucla/research/folklore.html that also leads to other sites involving folklore, Halloween, and the Day of the Dead.

9. Because these things were a rarity—most people didn't live long enough to get gray hair and, because of their tribal influence, had the same eye color or hair color—to be different was to be dead.

10. *Articles on Witchcraft, Magic and Demonology, Witchcraft in England,* edited by Brian P. Levak, University of Texas, Garland Publishing, Inc., 1992.

11. Hugh McLachlan and J. K. Swales, "Lord Hale, Witches and Rape," Ibid. The Elizabethan statute (1563) made the conjuration of evil spirits and killing by WitchCraft a capital offense. A year's imprisonment, with four appearances in the pillory, was the punishment for harm to the person or damage to property by WitchCraft and for a number of techniques associated with white Witches, which helped to lessen the growing death toll.

12. Rossell Hope Robbins, *The Encyclopedia of Witchcraft and Demonology,* Crown Publishers, 1959, page 538.

13. Walker, page 1041.

14. Ibid, pages 1068–1069.

15. D. L. Ashliman, "Werewolf Legends from Germany," *Index of Folklore and Mythology Electronic Texts,* 1997.

16. Philip and Stephanie Carr-Gomm, *The Druid Animal Oracle,* Fireside, 1994, page 77.

17. Ibid.

chapter

4

HALLOWEEN DIVINATIONS

Just a little witch
on high
She'll tell you that
your love is nigh
Your fortune on Hallowe'en
when told
My secret will the witch unfold.

—FROM AN EARLY NINETEENTH-CENTURY
HALLOWEEN POSTCARD

From our studies of tribal affairs throughout the world, we have discovered that the early peoples mixed mysticism and religion together and that, often, this combination governed the people. In our exploration of Halloween, we learned that the Paleopagans and the Celtic peoples used divination techniques to ascertain information for the good of the tribe on Samhain (summer's end). Divination procedures continued to figure in Celtic-Christian practices, ceasing on a governmental level around 1300 C.E.; however, there we find numerous historical accounts of royalty and peasantry using divination tools in secret after that period. During Queen Elizabeth's reign, the prominence of the practice was such that she specifically instituted laws to stop people from divining the hour of her death. She felt that divinations on that subject would put her governmental affairs in jeopardy, but didn't appear concerned over the religious ethical practice of fortunetelling.

During the Victorian era, Europe and America experienced a resurgent interest in divination techniques, though by then most of these activities had disintegrated into party games or were passed off as mere superstition. The Fox sisters began their foray into spiritualism and séances to talk to the dead in the 1930s, firing a fad that has undulated through American history since that time. By the 1960s in America, divination techniques sold as a service were outlawed by local ordinances in some areas, and on occasion state laws attempted to eradicate the practice, though in other, less biased areas such services continue to flourish. Virginia, a seat of colonial occult practices, gnawed viciously at its early roots, enacting stiff penalties for card readers and other types of occult practices. Although various local governments tried to eradicate divination-for-sale, the American appetite for such practices grew more ravenous with each passing year. Current sales on astrological techniques and divination practices remain a constant dollar maker as the American public searches for answers to age-old questions.

In this chapter we'll cover some of the early divination practices of the Paleopagans as well as more recent techniques, including scrying and psychometry.

The Casting of Lots

Most tribal divination systems began with the use of "lots" made of bone, shell, or wood. The tribal system had a finite number of lots; for example, four to twenty-four pieces. Four lots could conceivably give you sixteen combinations, each combination relating to a specific message. Each pattern may have its own sponsoring divinity, future meaning, present advice, and spiritual plan. A second throw would include an additional finite number of messages. The more lots, the more patterns, the more throws, the more extensive the answers. The closest I've seen to this lot system is a Santerian technique called *sortilege*. The current popular rune system with twenty-four disks, each with its own design (depending on the system you use), began with the lot system.

Although we may think that a system of four lots would be easy to read and take little time to learn, this is not the case, especially when all possible patterns (including double throws) were committed to memory. At the minimum we are talking one full year of intense study, and three years of study for intermediate accomplishment. So if you think that Celts sat around throwing a few bones for a simple answer, you are sadly mistaken.

Through the survival of sortilege and the runic system,[1] we see that several steps were taken by the magickal person before the lots were cast, including purification and prayer. The casting of lots was considered a very serious business, and the fun and games appearing in later Victorian practices at Halloween parties pale in comparison to these early divination techniques.

Yes/No Stones

For individuals who are not familiar with any divination technique, the yes/no stones are the easiest to master; however, the most difficult factors in using any divination techniques are not trusting your intuition and trying to second-guess the issue, and asking the proper question (wording your question in a clear and concise manner).

In any divination technique, the answer you receive indicates *what will most likely happen if you continue on your chosen path.* There are no demons, nasty critters, or bad old Satans moving the stones under your nose. Answers are culled from the collective human unconscious and tempered by divinity. Your fate is not fixed, nor is it carved in stone. Although I teach my children and students that there are no stupid questions in the world, stupid questions in divination will bring you stupid answers, and there are many questions that you could answer without a divination tool. For example, if someone sits down with me and asks for a reading, I usually ask them for a specific question. Focus, whether we are talking about divination or studying for an exam, should be your primary concern. If you ask me, "Will I ever lose weight?"— that is not a good question. I would then ask you, "Do you want to lose weight? If you want to, then you will; you don't need a divination tool for that answer." The same goes for "Will I ever get married?" Let's face it: statistically, you probably will, therefore that's not a good question either. Your marriage could be so far in the future that the present question truly isn't valid. A very good rule of broomstick is: Read only for the next six months.

Sometimes you will get the right answer to the question, but not the answer that you need. For example, I cast a simple yes/no lot with the following question: "Did I bring the present situation upon myself?" What I really wanted to know was: Did I directly cause the problem I was currently experiencing—but I didn't say that. The answer to my original question was "Yes." This was a dilemma for me because I could not see how I caused the situation that I thought had nothing to do with me in the first place. Rather than scooping up the lots and dumping them in a drawer, I sat quietly and contemplated the answer to my question. I realized that, indirectly, I had caused the problem—simply by being who I am. This wasn't a bad thing, just the honest answer. When I threw the lots again, rewording the question, I received the answer I needed to help me better understand the situation. I learned that I had not directly caused the situation, but the fact that I exist, and that I had been at a certain place at a certain time, brought the problem to my doorstep. From there, I could ask more questions and determine what would be best for me to do.

The final rule of broomstick when using any divination tool is not to depend on that tool for all your answers in life. A divination tool is just that—a tool, not God.

To make your own lots, choose three items of the same size: three small stones, three small pieces of wood, and so on. Paint one side solid or with a mark or a design. Leave the other side of the object blank. The painted side will mean a positive answer, the blank side will mean a negative answer. Hold the objects in your hands and ask your question in the manner that a yes or no answer would give you the information that you need. This isn't always as easy as it sounds, but once you get used to wording your questions, your answers will be clearer.

Close your eyes and ask Spirit (or whatever you see as divinity) to aid you in this divination. Ask your question, then throw the objects. Use the key below:

Three yes objects = Yes

Three no objects = No

Two yes objects and one no object = A struggle, but the conclusion will be "Yes." Throw again to determine the source of the struggle.

Two no objects and one yes object = Maybe, but the outcome has not been determined due to decisions that you, or someone else, will make. Throw again to learn more details.

Some individuals like to meditate first, and burn a candle while casting the yes/no lots. Try not to do your divination while you are rushed, as you won't be able to concentrate properly. Keep a record of your answers.

If you would like to expand your lots to include a timing mechanism, paint a fourth stone with a full moon on one side and a new moon on the other. You can throw this with the other three lots, or separately.

Circle of Ashes and Stones

There are many practices followed on Halloween Eve that don't fall into the lot system. These practices are "once and done" procedures that became superstition, but appear to be birthed by ritual or religious formulas. The earliest and most prevalent practices revolve around the bonfire and a white stone, and we can find records of this practice in Wales, Scotland, Ireland, and Britain. Each person takes a white stone, marks the stone, and buries it in the ashes of the bonfire. The person says a prayer and walks around the bonfire three times. In some areas, the young men of the family guard the stones, making a game out of protecting the "family jewels." When the teens and young adults tire of jousting, the smaller children take over and the emotional content around the practice grows more serious. Just as children were used to "watch the hearthfires" in Germany[2] and other Celtic regions to ensure warmth and cooking capabilities in the morning, here the little ones were responsible for the "lives" of each family member until dawn. If, the morning after the bonfire was reduced to cold ashes, any family member's stone is discovered missing, the superstition prevailed that the person who belonged to the missing stone would be dead before the next Halloween. In North Wales, this fire was called Coel Coeth, where each family built a separate bonfire near their homes. In Scotland, the ashes were collected from all the bonfires in the area, then spread into a large circle. Each person would hide their stone in the ashes of the big circle. The next morning a Druid priest would rekindle the main bonfire to ensure the health and wealth of those whose stones remained.

Apple Divinations

Apples have figured prominently in Pagan religious and magickal lore, which is probably why the early Christians made it the fruit of evil. The apple's history includes numerous accounts of sacred associations to goddess iconography, thus making it a perfect candidate for the Garden of Eden mythos. If we cut an apple in half, we find the five-pointed star (the pentacle), which is a positive magickal symbol meaning earth, air, water, fire, and the Spirit of the human. The people of Europe, however, were not about to give up their apples, despite the consternation of the early church, nor would they ignore the magickal folklore surrounding the fruit. In the British Isles, October 31 was known as Snap Apple Night, and a Cornish custom indicates that children were given a large apple on Halloween as a symbol of long life and happiness.

True love is the highest significance of the apple and we find numerous divinations throughout Halloween history that employ this forbidden fruit. Apples were thought to help you find a true love, or discover if your lover has been faithful (or not).

- If a girl stands before a mirror while eating an apple and combing her hair at midnight on Halloween, her future husband's image will be reflected in the glass over her left shoulder.

- If a girl cuts an apple into nine pieces at midnight on Halloween in front of a mirror, then sticks each piece with the knife and holds each piece (one at a time) over her left shoulder, as the ninth piece hits the reflection in the mirror, she will see her future husband.

- If a girl peels an apple in one long piece at midnight on Halloween, and then tosses the peel over her left shoulder or into a bowl of water, she will be able to read the first initial of her future partner's name in the shape assumed by the discarded peel.

- If a girl peels an apple at midnight on Halloween and hangs the peel on a nail by the front door, the initials of the first man to enter will be the same as those of her unknown lover.

- If a group of unmarried boys and girls each attach an apple to a string and twirl the apple over a fire, the order in which the apples fall off the string indicates the order in which they will all be married. The owner of the last apple to drop will remain unmarried.

- In a group of unmarried boys and girls, each person marks an apple and places it in a large bucket of water, along with unmarked apples. Without using their hands, the teens attempt to take bites out of the apples floating in the water. The teen is fated to marry the person whose apple they bite. Another variation of this custom consists of hanging the apples from strings tied to a tree.

- The American custom of apple bobbing does not mark the apples. Whoever snags an apple first will be wed first, and if a boy or girl puts the apple they caught during the bobbing game under their pillow on Halloween Eve, they will dream of their intended lover.

- For the girl who has many suitors, the apple seed divination is a must. The young woman peels an apple and places a wet seed named for each boyfriend on her cheeks. The seed to fall off last will be her next lover. Variations include sticking the seeds on the eyelids or forehead. The girl can also put the seeds in a heavy pan on the stove. The first seed to pop declares who will be (or is) unfaithful.

• For a suitor to declare his bravery for his lady love at a party, the young woman's apple is hung from a string on one side of a pole and a lit candle hung on a string on the other side of the pole. As the pole is spun amid cheers and laughter, the suitor must brave the flame to catch the apple in his teeth. If he fails to do so, the couple will not be a couple much longer.

As we can see, many of the practices slipped from the realm of divination and into the territory of party games—by the early 1900s no one really believed the divinations would work, but they presented such a delightful avenue for fun that the practices continued.

Water Divinations

Earth, air, water, and fire have always provided humans with access to the mystical realms involved in divination. Halloween Eve, as we've seen, was the night to delve into the unknown. Historically, water divinations appear popular during the harvest season. As with the apple divinations, water divinations began as a solo enterprise associated with Halloween, then eased into party games or activities to be done with group participation.

• If a young girl washes her undergarments on Halloween Eve and, without saying anything, hangs them over a chair to dry, she will (if she is awake long enough to see) watch the form of her future husband enter the room and turn the undergarments. One tale holds that a young girl in Scotland did this and instead of seeing her lover, saw a coffin. The next day she discovered that her lover had died.

• If a young woman goes to a lake at midnight on Halloween, and gazes at her image in the water, she shall see her lover's face reflected before her.

• A young girl should take three pails of water and place them in her bedroom on Halloween Eve, then pin her nightdress opposite her heart with three leaves of green holly. If she is roused from a deep sleep by the call of three bears, the sounds will die away, followed by a hoarse laugh. After the laugh ceases, the form of her future husband will appear. If he is deeply attached to her, he will change the position of the pails. If not, he will pass from the room without touching them.

- A young girl, on Halloween Eve, should dribble hot wax (or hot lead) into a cauldron filled with water to find the circumstances of her intended. If the shape resembles a ship, he will be a sailor, while a coffin means widowhood, and so on. "In the unique and feisty Massachusetts community of Marblehead, unmarried women customarily hung a pot of tallow over the fire, then dropped iron hobnails into the fat, believing their husbands-to-be would appear."[3]

- A surviving party game entails the use of three bowls and a blindfold. The first bowl is filled with clear water. The second bowl is filled with dirty water. The third bowl remains empty. The blindfolded person dips their hands into one of the bowls. If the bowl with the clear water is chosen, the blindfolded person will marry a virgin. If the bowl with dirty water is selected, then he or she will be widowed (or, depending on the game, will not marry a virgin). If the empty bowl is chosen, then the blindfolded person will not marry.

Another version of this game indicates that the clean water means the future partner will be attractive and a joy to be with; the dirty water means the prospective partner is married to someone else; and the empty bowl indicates no partner to be found at this time. An American variation of this game includes apples in the first bowl, nuts in the second, and soot in the third. If the apples are chosen, the individual will experience luck and love throughout the coming year (or throughout their life). If the nuts are chosen, the person will be quite fertile and have great strength and unchanging luck. If the blind-folded person chooses the bowl of soot, then they will experience loss of love or sickness in the coming year (or throughout their life).

Nut Divinations

The Celtic peoples believed that nuts held powerful magick, and in Britain October 31 was sometimes called Nut Crack Night. The early Celts gave offerings of hazel nuts and apples to the Samhain bonfires and hearthstone fires in hopes that the departed loved ones could eat the offerings on the Other Side. In America, chestnuts and walnuts were plentiful during harvest and figured prominently in popular divination games.

- A maiden gathers a handful of nuts and names each one for a potential suitor. On Halloween Eve she places all the nuts on a grate over the fire. If the nut burns true and does not move, the suitor will be faithful. If the nut moves or pops, the prospective lover will be unfaithful.

- A maiden gathers two nuts, one for herself and one for her suitor. On Halloween Eve she places them on a grate over the fire. If the nuts burn well together, then a long marriage and happiness is foretold. If, however, one nut darts sideways, the person the nut represents will stray and the other person is advised to seek a different mate.

Pumpkin Seed Divinations for Solitaries or Parties

With all the pumpkins you'll be carving this Halloween, be sure to set aside twenty-four large pumpkin seeds for this divination technique. The runes are a specific system of magickal writing and their age is about as old as the hills, meaning no one really knows how old they are. The cultures from which they sprang were wild, brazen, and strong, not refined like those of the Egyptians. Perhaps this is why the runes are so successful—they are uncorrupted by civilization.

There are twenty-four runes, and each has a corresponding phonetic sound, its own divinatory meaning, its own deity, and its own magickal use. In my personal opinion, the runes are far more powerful as a magickal vehicle than the tarot. They also mix exceedingly well with other tools.

The Germanic runes (those most familiar) are called the Elder Futhark. This is the entire sequence of the rune row in its fixed order, much like saying A B C D E, and so on. The Futhark is divided into three sections, called aettir or aett. Each section consists of eight runes in a fixed order.

The first tier deals with deities and their dominion, the second corresponds with necessary forces to bring about change, and the third deals with condition, usually human in nature.

To make your pumpkin runes, wash the seeds in a colander with cool water and allow them to dry thoroughly. With a fine-tipped black indelible felt marker, draw the rune signs shown below—one on each seed (on only one side). Hold the seeds over a dish of ice and ask for the blessings of water. Hold the seeds over a lit candle and ask for the blessings of fire. (Be careful—don't burn yourself.) Draw a circle the size of a dinner plate on a piece of poster board. Put the seeds in a colorful dish or pouch.

Formulate your question carefully. You can pull one pumpkin rune to determine the answer, or you can shake all the pumpkin runes in your hands and drop them on the poster board. Here are the rules:

- Seeds with the rune pattern up should be read. Seeds with the rune pattern not showing are not to be read (or can be read as hidden influences, but this takes longer).

- Runes close to the center of the circle show what is happening now. Runes farther away from the center show situations moving in or moving out of your life.

- Runes close together tell a story, and can be read much like a sentence. Runes far apart may not relate to the same situation.

- Runes outside the circle show forces that circle your life at this time. You can use these forces or discard them—this is your choice.

Feoh, Fe (Abundance)

This rune stands for the creative aspects of fire and is female in nature. It is invoked for love, war, and WitchCraft. A good fortune rune, it allows you to draw wealth to you and maintain it. Feoh is a rune of new beginnings and expansive energy. Used with a healing rune, it acts as a catalyst/energy source. Feoh carries her own warning, one of the need to share the good fortune that comes to us, or else it will either destroy us or leave us worse off than we were before. Excellent in bind runes[4] to bring in energy.

Ur (Strength)

The auroch is a now-extinct European bison that was considered extraordinarily ferocious. It is a masculine rune that corresponds to the fierce power of ice, as in the movement of the glaciers. Therefore, akin to a glacier, auroch moves with determination and purifies all it touches. Patience, courage, persistence, and strength are all qualities of this rune. It can be invoked for defense, crop fertility, good weather, strength, and healing. Excellent in bind runes for healing purposes.

Thuriasz, Thor (Opposition)

Thuriasz is seen as the force of opposition and chaos in the world and is the negative balance in the scales of nature. It is the shadow self of each person or positive deity. Thuriasz represents fire in its uncontrolled form and is the driving force behind a curse. Of all the runes, it is by far the most dangerous and can easily backfire. It was known as a war rune, one invoked to cause unmitigated fear and panic in the opponent. The rune Isa is used as a protective backdrop. But although extraordinarily destructive, it is also extremely protective. A ring of Thuriasz runes will keep out anything harmful or destructive.

Asa (Wisdom)

Asa is invoked for wisdom and occult knowledge from a higher, positive source. Its element is air and it is associated with the sacred breath. In Pow-Wow, Asa would be used during the faith healing process and is one of the runes that should be invoked by signing with the hand. It is often thought of as Odin's rune and has the highest vibration of the twenty-four runes. Asa represents intelligence and reason and therefore corresponds well to the written word and all sorts of messages. It is used in invisibility spells, for healing, and for cursing.

Radio (Travel)

Radio literally makes things go. It represents the act of being in charge and of motion and allows you to control particular situations. Where Feoh makes things go, Radio represents the directed pathway on which it will travel. The primary element of this rune is fire. Radio is invoked as a conduit for taking control and beginning new projects. It is also good for legal matters and protecting any type of machinery on wheels.

Kenaz (Breakthroughs)

Kenaz may be seen as the divine torch, bearing clarity of thought and insight. Kenaz is invoked for protection, teaching, love, war, and Witch-Craft. The element of fire in its beneficial form is shown here and is used in astral travel and to expose the hidden. Kenaz can be used as a weapon to get rid of unwanted influences.

Gebo (Gift)

The magickal connotation of Gebo is balance. It is the rune of partnership, whether you are speaking of two opposing or agreeing forces. Gebo is invoked to enhance exchange of data, ideas, or feelings. A rune of the element of air, it moves swiftly in many situations. It works well to bind two runes together and is used both in blessings and cursings. Gebo is the rune of honor and self-sacrifice.

Wunjo (Joy)

Wunjo is truly a happy rune, one of joy and happiness. It stands for blessings, fertility, gifts, light, and perfection. It is a fruitful rune and ensures proper payment for efforts extended. Wunjo is a harmonious rune. Combined with Radio, it will control and direct the will to a joyful conclusion. With Gebo, it brings one into harmony with divine will. The most beneficial aspect of Wunjo is the ability to exert one's will to facilitate wishes coming true.

Hagalaz (Change)

Hagalaz stands for the seed of ice and liberation through drastic means. It is disruptive and affects change. Invoked, it can create confusion and disruption, but it is also excellent in staving off astral attack. It is used for protecting barns or homes from storms. Hagalaz indicates a need for change, a journey into the underworld of the subconscious to bring about positive transmutation. Hagalaz is an interesting rune, for it can turn someone's past against them to hasten a positive change. This is the rune of Urd, the eldest sister of the Wyrd.

Nauthiz (Need)

Nauthiz is a good stress reliever as it allows you to reach deep inside yourself and bringing forth personal inspiration. Nauthiz is associated with Skuld, the third and youngest sister of the Wyrd. Runes that follow this one indicate what is needed in order to bring about the desired future. Nauthiz was considered a war rune, as its energies were used to stop and deflect incoming fire or magickal attack. To see Nauthiz in the world around you is an indication that a mistake has been made, a warning that there may be some unacknowledged needs to attend to.

Isa (Stop)

Isa is the rune of Verandi, the Wyrd sister who rules the present. She stops unrestrained growth and can freeze activity for a full three months, where the present situation is destined to remain the same for a short period of time. Isa is ice. Invoked, she is used to freeze another's action and can negate disruptive influences, whether they are magickal or physical in nature. Isa can be destructive by not allowing needed movement.

Jera (Harvest)

Jera represents harvest and is a cyclical rune of reward. It represents a gentle flow of change rather than one of fast pace. It is a friendly, smooth-moving rune, used for timing in magickal operations. It can be used to speed things up or slow things down. Jera's change is lasting and is effective for assisting those in great need.

Eihwaz (Endings)

Eihwaz stands for eternity and a world without time. It is a "go for it" rune but should not be used lightly due to its relationship to the Yew tree, the tree of death. Powerful in death spells, it is an excellent conduit for reaching ghostly realms and represents the Tree of Yggdrasil (the Tree of Life). Eihwaz is the rune of the hunter and can be invoked when searching for a person, place, or thing. It can also be used to find a job or a home. It is a good bind rune, providing it is used properly.

Perth (Secrets)

Perth is a rune of secrets and hidden knowledge and is the material used by the Norns to weave the tapestry of one's fate. It often foretells an initiation experience, rebirth, or a discovery of great import. Invoked, it is useful for contacting the Norns, for past-life regression work, and for divination. It is a good rune to contact the collective unconscious of the folk soul. Perth is a rune of psychic powers, childbirth, and marital fidelity, and is often explained as evolutionary process. Perth symbolism often appears when a great change is about to take place that has been hidden up to this point from the mind of its main participant.

Algiz (Protection)

Algiz is the main rune of protection. It acts as a powerful conductor and is said to represent the horns of a stag or elk. Invoked, Algiz is an excellent shield, from guarding letters through the postal system to protecting your home. It is also used when you fear a magickal working may have some unpleasant repercussions that you do not wish to deal with.

Sowilo (Success)

Sowilo is the sigil of the sun, navigation, and healing. Often its inspiration is from some type of divine source and the message that it brings is a needed one in order for you to reach your desired goals. Sowilo can be a slap in the face, indicating you were blinded by someone or something and now you need to wake up. Invoked, Sowilo is used in healing, to draw divine energy to the needed area or person.

Tiwaz (Justice)

Much like Maat in Egyptian symbology, Tiwaz is unperverted justice. Invoked for courage, honor, justice, dedication, and bravery in a difficult situation, Tiwaz lends justice to the deserving. Good when drawing up contracts and rules of play, and excellent in legal issues as a bind rune.

Birca (Beginnings)

Birca is the patron of mothers, children, and women's mysteries. It provides both emotional and physical security and is the rune of the mysteries of the Wyrd. Birca is a soft and maternal rune. Invoke Birca for childbirth, problems involving children and marital affairs, women's illnesses, and where things need to grow.

Ehwaz (Partnership)

Ehwaz is the symbol of the horseman or war horse. It is a rune that flows and adjusts to new issues or problems. Although often thought of as male in nature, it tends more to the female energies. Invoked, Ehwaz can bring people together or split them apart. It allows one to take control of a situation or issue and can create links for good or ill.

Mannaz (Destiny)

Mannaz is a people rune. It deals with the cooperation between people for a beneficial end and with the thought process of humanity, where it eventually falls to verbal, written, or legal form. Mannaz often deals with your life mission or your career. Invoked, it can provide an intellectual edge over an opponent. As a bind rune with Perth and Eihwaz, it is useful in contacting the dead.

Laguz (Flow)

Laguz is the rune of flow and sorcery and is used to gain access to someone's mind, to send thoughts, and to facilitate mutual feelings. Its element is water and its gender is feminine. Invoked, it enables one to form things by visualizing with ease, attracting a love interest, and healing or visiting someone in dreamtime to talk seriously and honestly with them about a particular issue of mutual concern.

Inguz (Passion)

Inguz is a type of fertile, magick circle. It contains strong foundations and room to grow. As a bind rune, it is used as a vessel of gestation, whereas the other runes are placed inside the vehicle of Inguz. Invoked, Inguz is a doorway to the astral yet provides the necessary grounding for the journey. Inguz is a cyclical rune, where sowing, nurturing, and growth are evident.

Dagaz (Transformation)

Dagaz is a rune that indicates a breakthrough of exciting proportions. It marks the end of a cycle or era and the promise of something new and better. Dagaz is a catalyst rune in an uplifting and happy sense. Invoked, this rune brings light and transformation into a situation. It can also be used as a rune of protection and to hide things in the astral and the physical. Dagaz is mysterious and is said to render the wearer invisible. Placed at the four quarters of a magick circle, your work will go unnoticed by outside interference.

Othala (Roots)

Othala deals with ancestral property, both physical and nonphysical, as well as one's heritage. Invoked, Othala brings ancestral power and supports values and traditions of the family. Othala gives access to the universal folk soul and provides a sense of togetherness. It is also used in centering either an issue or one's self.

Blank Rune (Unknown)

Even a novice can use the runes for divination—just remember to stick to the key words (in parentheses after the rune) and you'll be fine. Those who find the runic system intriguing, and wish to study this ancient technique fully, should check the suggested reading list at the back of this book.

Contemporary Halloween Party Lots

One doesn't always have to be serious with a game of lots, and if you like you can make the questions up ahead of time or allow the participants to think up their own questions. Here's a game to keep the laughter rolling at your next Halloween party!

- 1 bag dried beans
- 2 decorated boxes
- A black marker
- 50 slips of paper

Divide the beans in half. On one half of the beans, use a black marker to make an X on both sides of the bean. Mix all the beans together in one of the decorated boxes. Now take fifty or more slips of paper and, in black marker, write a silly question on each paper. Fold each paper and place in the other decorated box.

Beans marked with an X are "yes" beans. Those not marked are "no" answers. Turn out all the lights and sit in a circle with a candle or two glowing in the darkness. Put both boxes in the center of the circle. Each person has to draw a question, ask it aloud, then draw a bean. They must tell the group their answer, and return the bean to the box. Throw the question away. Since this is a game, the questions can be as serious or as silly as you like. After you run out of questions, pass the box of beans around the circle. Each person is to ask a serious question of their own, and draw a bean to discover the answer. The serious question is to remind the participants of the legacy of drawing lots.

Making a Magick Mirror

Scrying (seeing into the future using a mirror, crystal ball, or other glass object) is such an old practice that no one knows when the tradition first began. Typically, the crystal ball or magick mirror remained the chosen favorite. In the past thirty years, with the new technologies in glass processing, many magickal practitioners have turned to artificially manufactured "crystal" balls. You can purchase a manmade scrying ball for a reasonable price. I think I spent eighteen dollars on the stand and twenty-eight dollars on the ball. Although some purists in the magickal community argue that manmade glass balls do not work well, the same number of individuals have experienced great success with these processed globes. Magick mirrors, on the other enchanted hand, are less expensive, requiring only the price of a convex glass, black enamel paint, and a selection of herbs. For you history buffs, forty years ago, the magick mirror was called a speculum.

- 1 convex piece of glass (an old clock face works well)
  A wooden circle the size of the clock face
  Black enamel paint
  Mortar and pestle
  Eyebright (herb)
  Wormwood (herb)
- 1 glass jar
- 1 cup spring water
- 1 small black cloth (a black napkin will do)
  Cheesecloth or a coffee filter
  Glue

Clean the glass. Paint two coats of black enamel on the convex side of the glass. Paint both sides of the wooden circle with two coats of black enamel. (You can use spray paint—just be very careful you don't create any drips.) Allow to dry thoroughly. Crush the wormwood and eyebright in the mortar with the pestle. Pour one cup of spring water into the glass jar. Add the herb mixture. Cover with black cloth. Let stand for twelve hours. Using cheesecloth, strain and dispose of the herbs. Paint over the enamel with the spring water mixture three times. Allow to dry thoroughly between applications. Glue the glass onto the wooden disk. Let dry.

Making a Scrying Vehicle

Whether you use a crystal or glass ball or employ a magick mirror on Halloween Eve for scrying, you need to collect some supplies and prepare the vehicle.

2   black tablecloths
    A yellow placemat cut into a triangle, twelve inches each side
    Morgana's incense mixture or other clearing and purifying incense
1   white candle (for Spirit)
1   purple candle (for speaking to the dead)
    Pencil and a pad of paper (for keeping record of your questions
      and answers; at a party, you may wish to use a tape recorder)

Place a black tablecloth on the table you intend to use for scrying. Set the yellow triangle in the middle of the table. Put your magick mirror or glass ball in the center of the triangle. This triangle represents spiritual protection. (If you want to be really snazzy, you can embroider a yellow triangle on the tablecloth and dispense with the plastic rendition.) Light the incense and pass the smoke over the candles and the divination tool, asking the energies of air to exorcise, consecrate, and bless your vehicles (tools) for divination.

To prepare a crystal or glass ball, wash thoroughly, then pass the ball over fire and ice, asking for the exorcism, consecration, and blessing of Spirit, then follow the directions below for either the ball or your magick mirror.

Hold the white candle tightly in your hands and ask Spirit to exorcise and bless the candle. Light the white candle, asking for the presence of divine Spirit. If you will be talking to the dead, perform the same technique with the purple candle, but do not light the candle at this time.

Hold your hands over the magick mirror or crystal ball and ask Spirit to exorcise and bless this vehicle of divination, this portal to the world of the unseen. Seal the blessing by drawing an equal-armed cross in the air over the divination tool, saying "So mote it be." Snuff out the candle, remove the burning incense, and cover the table with the second black tablecloth, protecting the ball or mirror until you are ready to use the divination tool.

On Halloween Eve, remove the protective black tablecloth and set aside. There are a few rules in scrying:

- Scry in a quiet place, without threat of interruption.
- If you are doing this at a party, use a separate room so that the happy guests do not distract you.
- Do not ask silly questions.
- Do not ask to speak to someone you don't know. Stick to Spirit or a deceased person who held only unconditional love for you.
- You can scry in a fully lit room, but some people require reduced lighting or only the light of the Spirit candle. I have found it easier to use only the candle light, as bright lights distract me.
- If you wish to speak to the dead, please read chapter 7 thoroughly first.

When you are ready to scry, light the incense and say:

In the name of Hecate

Great lady of the crossroads

I summon forth thy gift of far sight

From your lips to my ears

Bring forth the information I require

Blessings upon us this hour.

So mote it be.

If you wish to gain information from a specific loved one, call out his or her name three times, and then light the purple candle. Sit quietly, take a deep breath, and relax. If you wish to speak to a deceased loved one, you may find it helpful to have an article of clothing or a piece of jewelry that belonged to them. If you can't find either of these articles you could place his or her favorite flower on the table.

Every time you ask a question, pass the incense over the ball or mirror in an equal-arm cross motion both before you ask the question and after you have received the answer. Begin by saying:

> *I call forth my guardian angel*
>
> *to act as guide and protector this Halloween Eve*
>
> *Blessings of the Spirit upon you*
>
> *Speak to me* (the person's name, or just say Great Spirit—
>
> magickal people may wish to intone the name of an archetype).

Then ask your question. Be honest and ask your questions from the heart (no fooling around!). Gaze into the ball or mirror. Your vision will begin to tunnel, and you may perceive a mist moving over the divination vehicle. Sometimes the mist clears and you will see flashing pictures in your mind. Very rarely does one see an actual "picture" in the glass. I warn you that scrying takes practice, so you might want to experiment first before you make scrying the main event for your Halloween party. Once you have received information, write it down. It doesn't matter if the information doesn't make sense. You can contemplate the meaning later, not now. If you engage your analytical mind, you may not get any answers at all. When you have finished, thank Spirit, your guardian angel and, if you called a deceased loved one, send blessings and love to him or her, giving the loved one license to depart. Cleanse the divination vehicle one last time with the incense, then pass it over the fire. Say:

> *This session is over.*
>
> *Hail and farewell.*

Snuff out both candles. You can use the candles again for the same purpose, but do not use these candles for any other magickal or mundane operation. Some magickal individuals sprinkle the vehicle with holy water that they have gotten from the Catholic Church or made themselves. Wrap the divination tool in both black tablecloths and store in a plastic bag in a safe place with the candles and the yellow triangle.

Psychometry

Psychometry is the art of holding an object and identifying what information you receive from that object. All material things pick up psychic impressions of the people or animals that have either held or touched the object. Practicing psychometry can be great fun at a Halloween party or Samhain ritual. Remind each guest to bring an item that has an unusual history attached to it. Suggest that the histories be pleasant if you are dealing with nonmagickal guests. Place the items on a black cloth where they will not be disturbed until you are ready to relate your psychic impressions. You can lower the lights to set a calm and peaceful mood. You may play soft music in the background. Here are the rules to give to your guests before you begin. Please read the instructions first before trying this exercise. Remember, everyone is to get a turn.

- Everyone must be quiet while an individual is practicing psychometry. No whispering, laughing, or cracking jokes. Anyone who is not serious about using psychometry can leave the room.

- Hold the item lightly in your hand. Close your eyes and take a deep breath.

- Relax and take your time. You may need several minutes to feel calm and lock into information. You may see flashes in your mind, or your imagination might take you on a journey. Go with it.

- Say whatever comes to mind. Don't analyze. The other guests can do that later.

- When someone is practicing psychometry, say "That's right" the first time they hit on a correct statement. This gives the holder a psychological assurance to continue. Say nothing further and allow the "holder" to finish. Some individuals will be hesitant and say only one or two things, where others might give numerous impressions. The number of impressions received is not important.

- When you are done, say, "I'm finished," and pass the object to the next person.

- When the next person says something new that is correct, say, "That's right" and allow them to continue.

- When everyone has given his or her impressions of the object, the owner stands up and gives the complete history of who the object belonged to, what that person was (or is) like, and any information surrounding a pertinent event that involved the object.

Summary

In this chapter we've explored several divination vehicles, covering simple techniques and some of the more complicated vehicles. We do have a few general rules for divination, which we should cover before you test your hand at foretelling the future.

- A divination tool is only a vehicle. The tool is not possessed by any odd, grotesque entity. The vehicle contains only what you put into the tool.

- A divination tool tells you only what will most likely happen if you continue on your present path. If you choose to take a different path, then the outcome of the situation will be different.

- Do not live solely on information given by the divination tool. Use your free will and common sense.

- Never, ever say bad things to another person about his or her future. Divining carries a great responsibility on your part. Do not abuse the tool. If you do, you will reap exactly what you sow.

- If you cannot answer the question posed, then tell the truth. It is far better to say, "I don't know," than to make something up, fearing that you will look foolish. The honest diviner will be truly blessed in the future. The dishonest diviner will pay dearly for his or her journey into a self-gratifying ego trip.

- Be especially careful when speaking to the dead. They are dead, they are not God; therefore, they don't know everything. Do not contact individuals who were not truthful in life, even if they loved you more than life itself, and never try to contact anyone who had a history of abuse, criminal behavior, or mental dysfunction. The only exception here would be an Alzheimer's patient, who will retain his or her original faculties after death.

- If you treat the process of divination with respect, you will reap great rewards. If you treat the technique as a joke, you will glean nothing of the truth.

- Do not analyze your answers until you have finished with the reading. If you are working alone, I suggest taping the reading so that you won't have to interrupt yourself to write down the information you receive.

Divination can be a rewarding and useful process, assisting in goal planning, problem solving, and raising your self-esteem. I suggest that you work with several divination tools until you find the practice that works best for you. I also urge continual study on the subject, as there will always be opportunities to add to your education.

Notes

1. There are several other systems, but I'm using these two as examples only.
2. Wilhelmina Keefer, personal interview, 1992.
3. Marion L. Starkey, *The Devil in Massachusetts*, Doubleday/Anchor, 1969, pages 34-35.
4. Bind rune: Drawing several runes together, making a unique pattern for a particular magickal act.

chapter
5
HALLOWEEN IN THE KITCHEN

Double, double toil and trouble;
Fire burn and cauldron bubble. . . .
Eye of newt, and toe of frog,
Wool of bat, and tongue of dog,
Adder's fork, and blind-worm's sting,
Lizard's leg, and howlet's wing,
For a charm of powerful trouble,
Like a hell-broth boil and bubble.

—WILLIAM SHAKESPEARE,
"MACBETH"

99

Halloween wouldn't be complete without the "goodies" part. Whenever you prepare any food, here are some magickal rules of thumb:

- Stir counterclockwise to banish negativity from the food.
- Stir clockwise to instill good wishes of harmony, peace, and love.
- Add seasonings not only for their taste and nutrient value, but for their magickal correspondences as well.[1]
- When completed, empower the dish with love, health, and wealth energies by holding your hands over the dish, humming what you wish to instill until the palms of your hands tingle or grow warm.

General Ingredient Blessing

Put your hands over the ingredients of any dish. Envision pure, white light entering the ingredients. Circle your palms five times over the ingredients, and say:

From the east, the air brings wisdom

From the south, the fire brings creation

From the west, the water brings love

From the north, the earth brings stability

From the center, Spirit brings blessings.

Tap the kitchen counter three times, and say:

The love is sealed.

Cooking Blessing

Put your hands over the simmering pot, and repeat three times:

Three angels came from the east

Bringing blessings upon this feast.

The first said, "I banish all negativity."

The second said, "May you never thirst."

The third said, "May you never hunger."

In the name of the three

So mote it be.

With your hand (or a wooden spoon) make the sign of the equal-armed cross (see illustration above) over the cooking pot, then tap the spoon or your fingers lightly on the stove, saying:

This work is sealed.

Blessings of Vesta upon us.[2]

Samhain Serving Blessing

Hold your hands over the cooked food, and say:

The golden rays of sun kissed the grain

Sweet drops of rain caressed the fruit.

Streams of moonlight danced in the fields

Sending energy into the root.

Blessings of the Mother

Strength of the Father

Unity of Love.

So mote it be.

Make the sign of the equal-armed cross over the dish. Tap the dish once. Serve with a smile!

All Souls' Day Bread Recipe

In Cleveland county, England, loaves of bread, called Sau'mas Loves, were made for distribution among the children and the poor. Sets of square farthing cakes with currants in the center, commonly given by bakers to their customers, were kept in the house for good luck throughout the coming year. Some of the more prosperous individuals in Lancashire and Herefordshire gave cakes of oaten bread to the poor, saying "God have your soul, beens and all."[3] In Warwickshire seedcakes, much like rolls, were given as gifts to the inhabitants of the county. From Scotland, we have a large cake in the form of a triangle. Leave a small portion of All Souls' Bread outside for the faeries, and a portion at the cemetery or on your altar for the dead.

- 4   yeast cakes (fertility and money)
- 2   cups milk
- 8   cups flour (fertility and money)
- 1   teaspoon salt (protection)
- 8   egg yolks (fertility)
- 2   cups sugar (love)
- 1   teaspoon grated orange peel (love and money)
- 1   teaspoon grated lemon peel (protection)
- ½   cup butter
- 1   teaspoon poppy seeds (luck and invisibility)

Dissolve yeast in ½ cup milk, and add 1 cup of flour. Sprinkle a little flour on top and let rise until size doubles. Add salt and egg yolks, beat until thick. Add sugar and peels and mix with other ingredients. Add 2 cups flour and remaining milk, alternating each so that the mixture doesn't get too dry or too wet. Knead for 5 to 10 minutes, saying:

Blessings upon the living.

Prayers for the dead.

Hum if you like, or simply chant. Add remaining flour and butter, and knead until dough comes away from hands. Set dough in a warm place, covered with a warm, damp cloth, until it rises to double in bulk. Separate into 4 parts, braid. Brush top with beaten egg yolks and sprinkle with poppy seed. Let rise. Bake at 350 degrees for 1 hour.[4]

Pumpkin Bread

The pumpkin belongs to American culture and therefore carries no European magickal history. The pumpkin is considered feminine, ruled by the moon, with its element seen as water. Its magickal associations are protection and abundance of the harvest. Without a European connection, we have no European deity to fairly associate with this wonderful vegetable, though I'm sure any harvest deity would be amicable to the association.

1¾ cups all-purpose flour (fertility and money)

1½ cups sugar (love and passion)

¾ teaspoon salt (protection)

1 teaspoon baking soda

½ teaspoon ground cinnamon (spirituality and protection)

½ teaspoon ground nutmeg (luck and health)

1 cup canned pumpkin (abundance)

⅓ cup water (cleansing)

2 large eggs (fertility)

1 teaspoon vanilla (love and mental prowess)

½ cup vegetable oil

½ cup chopped walnuts (health and wishes—will counteract a fertility spell)

Confectioners' sugar

Combine all dry ingredients in a large bowl. Mix well. In a different bowl, combine pumpkin, water, eggs, vanilla, and oil. Mix well. Add dry ingredients slowly and beat thoroughly. Stir in nuts and pour batter into a greased loaf pan. Bake at 350 degrees for 75 to 80 minutes (but watch your time as different ovens may lengthen or shorten required time). Cool 15 minutes before removing from pan. Sprinkle with confectioners' sugar. Makes 1 loaf.

Harvest Pumpkin Pie

This quick pie can be made even by noncooks like me! Serve with whipped cream on top.
Display with dried Indian corn or dried corn husks.

 1 (9-inch) frozen pie shell (cauldron of transformation)
 3 eggs (fertility)
 1 (16-ounce) can pumpkin (abundance)
 ¾ cup brown sugar (love)
 1 teaspoon cinnamon (spirituality and protection)
 ½ teaspoon nutmeg (luck and health)
 1 teaspoon pumpkin pie spice (spirituality)
 1 cup evaporated milk
 ½ cup chopped pecans, optional (money and employment)

Preheat your oven to 350 degrees. Take frozen pie shell out of the freezer and leave at room temperature for about 10 minutes. Prick bottom and sides of the pie shell with a fork. Put into the oven to bake for about 3 to 5 minutes. Take pie shell out of the oven and cool for about 15 minutes. Leave the oven on.

Put eggs in large mixing bowl. Beat with a fork, whisk, or rotary beater until eggs are frothy. Open the can of pumpkin and add to eggs; add brown sugar, cinnamon, nutmeg, and pumpkin pie spice. Mix with spoon until blended. Add evaporated milk and stir again.

Sprinkle pecans on the bottom of the pie shell. Pour pie mixture over nuts. Increase oven temperature to 400 degrees and bake for 25 minutes. Lower temperature back to 350 degrees and bake another 15 minutes. Take pie out of oven and cool for 1 hour. Serves 8.

Divination Doughnuts

These doughnuts have a wonderful surprise in them for your Samhain guests. You can use them for a regular Halloween party or in ritual for communion. Take one doughnut and a bowl of milk and set outside on Halloween Eve as an offering to your local sidhe (devas or faeries).

- 1   egg, beaten (fertility)
- ½   cup brown sugar (love)
- ¾   cup molasses (love)
- ½   cup sour cream (protection)
- 3   cups all purpose flour (fertility and money)
- ¾   teaspoon baking soda
- 2   teaspoons baking powder
- ¾   teaspoon salt (protection)
- 2   teaspoons allspice (protection)
- 1   large container of vegetable oil
-     A heavy pot
- 1   roll of paper towels
- 17   fortunes written on small slips of paper (keep the fortunes positive and upbeat)

In a large bowl, blend egg, brown sugar, molasses, and sour cream. Sift in the dry ingredients and mix well. Chill for 2 to 3 hours. Pour oil into heavy pot. Heat to approximately 365 degrees. On a lightly floured board, roll out the dough, a small amount at a time, until the dough is ½-inch thick. Cut out the doughnuts with a 3-inch floured doughnut cutter. (If you don't have a doughnut cutter, use a cleaned tin can.)

Fry the doughnuts for 2 to 3 minutes or until golden brown, turning once during the cooking process. Drain the doughnuts on paper towels. Cut a small slit in each doughnut and insert the fortune. Sprinkle doughnuts with powdered sugar or other topping. Makes approximately 18 doughnuts.

Green Man Cake

Serve garnished with antlers and autumn leaves.

3 ounces unsweetened chocolate (love and protection)
1 stick butter
2 cups sugar (love)
3 eggs (fertility)
1 teaspoon vanilla (love and mental prowess)
1 teaspoon green food coloring (healing and abundance)
2¼ cups all-purpose flour (fertility and money)
2 teaspoons baking soda
1 cup sour cream (protection)
1 cup boiling water (cleansing)
Cooking spray
1 container frosting (your choice)
Decorative candy (candy corn, chocolate candies, and so on)
2 (9-inch) round cake pans
One set of real or decorative antlers; leaves for decoration

Preheat oven to 350 degrees. Melt chocolate in small saucepan over low heat. Allow to cool. Put butter, sugar, and eggs in a large mixing bowl. Beat with electric mixer on medium speed until light and fluffy. Add vanilla and the melted, cooled chocolate. Add green food coloring. Beat on low speed for about 1 minute until batter is blended.

Sift flour and baking soda into second bowl. Add to batter alternately with sour cream, mixing with long wooden spoon. Add boiling water to batter and mix again. Batter will be runny.

Spray bottom of baking pans with cooking spray. Lightly flour. Pour batter into pans and bake for about 35 minutes. Cool for 15 to 20 minutes. Frost and decorate.

Prosperity Pumpkin Raisin Muffins

This recipe is from Morgana of Morgana's Chamber in New York City. The recipe can be halved, and the muffins freeze well, too.

2	cups canned pumpkin purée (abundance)
1½	cups honey (riches)
4	eggs (or 8 egg whites if you want low fat)
1	cup evaporated skimmed milk (goddess symbolism)
1	cup water (element of water and the flow of prosperity)
1	tablespoon oil
1	tablespoon cinnamon (success)
1	teaspoon nutmeg (antihunger)
1	teaspoon ginger (money)
⅓	teaspoon ground cloves (money)
3½	cups whole wheat flour (abundance)
1	tablespoon baking soda
2	tablespoons baking powder
1	cup black raisins (money)

Mix the first ten ingredients in a large bowl. In another bowl, mix together the flour, baking soda, and baking powder. Add to wet ingredients all at once, whisking until blended (do not overmix). Stir first counterclockwise (widdershins) to banish poverty, then clockwise to pull in abundance and prosperity. Stir in raisins. Fill nonstick muffin pans to the top. Bake in a 350-degree oven for 30 to 35 minutes. Cool for 15 minutes before removing from pan. Batter can also be baked in two nonstick loaf pans for 60 to 65 minutes. Makes 2 dozen muffins.

Toasted Pumpkin Seeds

Note: Adult supervision required. Pumpkin seeds are excellent for Halloween spellwork and Halloween munching. If you designed the jack-o'-lantern protection totem (page 135), you've got plenty of pumpkin seeds. Some pumpkin seed recipes call for boiling the seeds first, where others do not. Although we boil them in this recipe, if you're in a hurry, you can skip that step—just be sure you've cleaned the seeds thoroughly before baking them.

Pumpkin seeds (wishes)
2 quarts water (purification)
½ cup salt or to taste (protection)
2 tablespoons olive oil (healing and peace)
2 tablespoons dried rosemary (protection)

Rinse pumpkin seeds. Boil water. Add salt. Pour seeds into boiling water. Boil until seeds are soft. (They should turn brownish-gray and many will slip to the bottom of the pot.) Drain the boiled seeds in a colander, and pat seeds dry. Put in a bowl with olive oil, salt, and the rosemary. Mix lightly. Preheat your oven to 350 degrees. Spread the seeds on a large cookie sheet covered with aluminum foil. Make a single layer of seeds (don't have any little piles). Put seeds in oven for 20 to 30 minutes. If the seeds turn brown, you are overcooking them. They should look white and dry. You do not need to turn the seeds. When finished, use a spatula to slide the seeds off the foil and into a bowl. Allow to cool before little hands touch them.

Witches' Brew

The offering of wine, ale, water, cider, or other fruit juice used for religious symbolism dates back to Paleopagan times. As an example, in Scotland on Samhain Eve (relating to the Isle of Lewis), inhabitants would take a chalice of ale brewed for the occasion and enter the sea up to their waists. There, they would speak the words of invocation to the God/Goddess of the sea, asking for blessings and protection, and then pour the contents of the chalice into the waters. Even during the early Christian era, this practice remained alive—the priest offering the ale to the mysterious power of the ocean and, of course, unto the God whom they believed created those seas.

If you would like to design a ritual for yourself along the lines of the sacred communion, you may wish to make the brew listed below. Apple cider has long been used as a libation to the Earth Goddess and deity in general. The apple (prized food of the unicorn) brings health, love, and wisdom to those who taste its enchanting juices.

- 1   gallon apple cider (love)
- 1   orange (love)
- 1   apple (love)
- 3   cinnamon sticks (love and psychic powers)
- ⅛   teaspoon nutmeg (fidelity)
- 1   handful rose petals (love)
- 1   big pot

Pour apple cider into a large kettle. Peel orange and squeeze its juice into cider, discarding the pulp. Tear the orange peel into 1-inch strips, and add to mixture. Core apple and cut into ¼-inch slices. Add to mixture. Break the cinnamon sticks in half. Add to mixture. Add nutmeg. Warm over low heat for 2 hours. Do not bring to a boil. Stir often, saying:

> *From the moon to the vine*
> *From the vine to the fruit*
> *From the fruit to this brew*
> *May the Lady send her blessings*
> *May the Lord grant your desires.*

Serve warm from pumpkin punch bowl, next page. Sprinkle with rose petals.

Pumpkin Punch Bowl

In magickal traditions, the cauldron represents purification and transformation. Use a pumpkin to represent your cauldron at your next Samhain ritual or for that great Halloween party.

2　glow-in-the-dark sticks
1　large pumpkin (abundance)
1　heat-resistant punch bowl that will fit inside the pumpkin (cauldron of transformation)

Hollow out pumpkin, and carve a design in it. Place punch bowl inside pumpkin. Right before the party begins, activate the glow-in-the-dark sticks per package instructions and place between pumpkin shell and bowl. Add enchanted Witches' brew!

Easy Enchanted Punch

Keep your party safe and sober by using this great nonalcoholic punch recipe.

8　cups cranberry juice (health and love)
6　cups apple cider (love)
6　cinnamon sticks (psychic powers)
6　orange slices (luck)
1　liter ginger ale (success)
1　tray of ice cubes

Pour cranberry juice and apple cider into a large bowl. Break the cinnamon sticks in half. Put one cinnamon stick and one piece of orange in each cube holder. Fill an ice cube tray with some of the cranberry-apple mixture. Freeze. Refrigerate remaining punch mixture in bowl. Before serving, add ginger ale and ice cubes.

Mozelle's Party Pumpkin

My mother, Mozelle Strader, was born in Buckhannon, West Virginia, and grew up on Pocahontas Street. She was the primo party thrower, coming up with amazing ideas on a shoestring budget. No one could outmaneuver her when it came to party ideas. Here's what you need for this terrific Halloween edible centerpiece that has been a tradition in my house for over forty years.

   Note: It takes approximately one hour to "dress" the pumpkin. This is something for the kids to do while you're running around with other preparations.

     An assortment of block cheeses
     Ring bologna—sweet, plain, and garlic
1   can pitted black olives (protection)
1   jar pitted green olives (healing)
1   jar small, sweet gerkins (healing)
2   boxes round toothpicks
1   medium-sized pumpkin (abundance)

Cut the cheese and bologna into ½-inch blocks. Put a piece of cheese or bologna on a toothpick. Top with olive or pickle. Insert the free end of the toothpick into the pumpkin. Continue this procedure until your pumpkin is covered with these fun party snacks!

Angel's Dreams and Wishes Pumpkin

Note: *I advise using this treat for adults only. This Halloween sweet treat follows some-what the same procedure as above, but found a new twist in the mind of my eighteen-year-old daughter.*

- 1 can Sterno cooking fuel
- 1 medium-sized pumpkin (abundance)
- 2–3 bags large marshmallows (dreams)
- 1 bag large gumdrops (wishes)
- 1 box toothpicks

Carve a hole in the top of the pumpkin that matches the size of the Sterno can. You want the Sterno can to fit snugly in the top of the pumpkin. (If you make the hole too big, don't despair—wrap the can with tin foil.) Insert Sterno can. Put one marshmallow on a toothpick, and stick the free end of the toothpick in the pumpkin. Intersperse with the large gum drops. Cover pumpkin with the marshmallows and gum drops. When the party begins, light the sterno. Guests can roast their own marshmallows. (Don't roast the gum drops.)

Candied Love Apples

Samhain is sometimes called "Feast of the Apples" as these luscious fruits have a histor-ical significance as food for the dead. Earlier in this book, we learned that the Celts fed apples to Samhain fires to spiritually empower their beloved dead, or buried the fruit in honor of a special loved one. The apple has long been a symbol of immortality, lust, and love. Perhaps the oldest apple spell consists of cutting an apple in half and sharing it with the person you wish to entice.

- 3 cups sugar (love)
- 1 cup light corn syrup (abundance and love)
- 1½ cups water (purity)
- 1½ teaspoons red food coloring (passion)
- 12 Popsicle sticks
- 12 medium apples (love and passion)
- 1 cup chopped peanuts, optional (fertility)

Combine sugar, syrup, water, and food coloring in sauce pan. Cook over medium heat until the mixture looks like wet cracks (8 to 10 minutes). Turn heat to low. Stick a popsicle stick into each apple (at the stem), and dip each apple into the sauce pan. Roll in peanuts. Place apples on waxed paper to cool and harden. Hold your hands over the apples, and say:

I conjure thee, O sweet fruit of love and immortality

To bring to those who touch or eat thee

Many blessings in love and wisdom.

Keep your hands over the apples until your palms grow warm. Be sure you tell your guests that they are eat-ing enchanted apples—we certainly don't want to cheat.

Baked Harmony Apples

These scrumptious apples will add harmony wherever they are served!

- 8 McIntosh apples (love and passion)
- 1 cup brown sugar (love and lust)
- 10 tablespoons chopped raisins (fertility and abundance)
- 1 stick butter, cut into small pieces
  Ground cinnamon (success and love)
  Ground nutmeg (health and fidelity)
- 2 cups water
- 2 cups dry white wine (fertility and passion)

Wash apples. Core the apples on one end. Mix together the brown sugar, raisins, and butter. Place the apples in a baking dish, cored end up, fill them with the brown sugar mixture, and then sprinkle the tops with cinnamon and nutmeg. Preheat the oven to 350 degrees. In a separate bowl, add the water to the wine. Hold your hands over the wine water, and say:

From the autumn sun to the vine

From the vine to the wine

I bless and empower this mixture

In the name of harmony.

Pour around apples. Bake for 45 minutes, basting occasionally. Serve with vanilla ice cream or whipped cream sprinkled with cinnamon. Serves 8.

Frosted Grapes and Honeyed Apples

Grapes have been used in fertility and money magick for centuries, and fall under the auspices of the moon; their element is water. A Samhain altar garnished with grapes is supposed to bring health, fertility, and material abundance. Magickally, honey is used to draw good things toward you or sweeten a situation. Apples, of course, represent love, passion, and lust.

1	large bunch of grapes (love and abundance)
1	egg white (fertility and protection)
½	cup of sugar (love)
6	apples (love and lust)
	Lemon juice (protection)
	Water
	Honey (love)
	Serving platter

Divide grapes into small clusters of about four or five grapes each. Put egg white into a small bowl. Whip until frothy but not stiff. Put sugar into another bowl. Dip each grape cluster first into the egg white, then into sugar, shaking off any excess sugar. Put grapes on paper towel to dry. Arrange grapes in the center of the platter. Just before serving, core apples and cut into slices. Arrange them in a circle around grapes. Sprinkle with a mixture of lemon juice and water to keep the apples from turning brown. Serve with honey.

Roasted Corn on the Cob

The Corn Mother or Corn Goddess is considered a deity of plenty and fertility. The corn dolly figures prominently in two rituals, one at Samhain and one at Candlemas. Corn has been used by various religious systems in ritual to signify the bounty of the earth. The magickal uses of corn include protection, luck, and divination techniques. In American folklore, an ear of corn was placed in the baby's crib to ward against negativity, and ancient Mesoamerican peoples would toss loose corn in the air during rain ceremonies. At Samhain, corn stalks hung over the largest mirror in the house and over the front door were thought to bring good luck to all those residing in the house.

Preparing corn on the cob for a Samhain feast or Halloween party is a wonderful, magickal way to bring prosperity to your party guests. Your adventure begins at the grocery store or produce stand. Check the corn by looking at the tassel. If the tassel isn't too dry, then the corn should be good. You can also break a few kernels with your fingernail—if juice spurts, then the corn is fresh.

Bring the corn home and place on your altar or in the center of your kitchen table. Hold your hands over the corn and ask the corn goddess (or your version of deity) to bless this corn and bring health and prosperity to all who will consume the corn. Keep your hands over the corn until your palms grow hot.

Carefully peel back the husks from the corn without taking the husks off. Pull off the silk and discard. Replace the husks, smoothing them onto the cob. Tie the ends together with a strip of the husk or string. Hum the words "abundance" and "prosperity" as you work through the corn. Set the corn aside until one hour before you plan to grill it.

Soak the corn one hour before grilling. Prepare your grill outside, asking Vesta, the goddess of hearth fires, to bless the fire. Place the corn on a medium-hot grill and turn often for 15 to 20 minutes. Try not to overcook. You can also wrap the corn in tin foil to help control the heating process if you are very busy scurrying around the house getting ready for your party! You can use the dying embers of your grill for nut divinations or in a personal ceremony for the remembrance of the dead.

Prosperity Popcorn Balls

Spread the wealth around by giving your friends empowered prosperity popcorn balls with a special wish for a productive and enchanting New Celtic Year.

- 1½ cups sugar (love and passion)
- ⅔ cup apple cider (love and passion)
- ⅔ cup maple syrup (abundance)
- ½ cup butter
- 1½ teaspoons salt (protection)
- ¼ teaspoon vanilla (love)
- 4 cups warm popped corn (abundance)

Combine sugar, cider, syrup, butter, and salt in a large pot. Bring to a slow boil over low heat, stirring occasionally. Turn off heat and remove crystallized sugar from sides of pot with a wet pastry brush. Bring mixture to a boil over medium heat for 4 to 5 minutes. Turn to low heat and add vanilla. Turn off heat. When mixture cools slightly, hold your hands over the bowl or pan, and say:

Mother of the Corn

Blessings of the sun

Blessings of the rain

From the earth to your hands

May each bite bring prosperity.

Hum or chant the word "prosperity" as you pour mixture over popcorn. Mix well. Butter your hands and roll into balls. Place on waxed paper. Store in an airtight container.

Tuna Ghouls

My son dearly loves this recipe. If you can't find Halloween cookie cutters, use the shape of a gingerbread man and cut off the legs to make tuna ghosts. If you're really in a hurry, just cut them like regular sandwiches and tell everyone that you had originally made them ghosts, but they shapeshifted into regular sandwiches.

- 2 (8-ounce) cans white tuna, packed in water
- 3 tablespoons of salad dressing
- 2 tablespoons relish (healing)
- 20 slices wheat bread, crusts removed (fertility and money)
  Halloween cookie cutters
  Whipped cream cheese
- 5 black olives (protection)

Drain tuna and mix with salad dressing and relish in a bowl. Cut the bread with the cookie cutters (be sure to have two of each shape). Spread 10 slices of bread with the tuna mixture. Put the matching slice of bread on top. Spread the top of each ghoul with cream cheese. Use two slices of olive to make eyes. Makes 10 sandwiches.

Magickal Mice

For a different twist, you can pickle the eggs and create red mice for that special Halloween party!

6   eggs (fertility)
1   carrot (fertility)
24 whole cloves (protection)
12 pieces licorice shoestring candy (wishes)
12 lettuce leaves (protection and love)

Hard-boil eggs by boiling gently for 15 minutes for medium to large eggs (or 12 minutes for small eggs). Remove from stove. Run cold water over eggs until they are cool to the touch. Set aside for 20 to 30 minutes or refrigerate overnight.

To make mice, peel eggs and run them under cold water to remove excess shell. Slice eggs in half lengthwise and set them, cut side down, on wax paper. Wash and peel carrot. Cut 2 carrot slices, the size and thickness of a dime or nickel, to be ears for each mouse. Cut a pointed base in each slice, then stick points into egg just above the narrow end, which will be the mouse's face. Put 2 cloves into each mouse for eyes. Arrange on lettuce on platter. Add licorice tails.

Quick Ideas for Busy People

Let's face it: you've got a full-time job and a full-time kid. October brings requests for that special costume, going to parades, trick-or-treating, and holiday parties. Although you try to be supermom, superdad, superstep-person, or superguardian, something's got to give. Here are some quick treat ideas for school or home that may save the face you normally wear.

Witches' Flying Mix

This fun mix takes only five minutes to prepare, looks great on the table, and tastes terrific. Witches' flying mix was especially designed for working moms or guardians whose schedules are jammed and who can't make something for the school party, or for the mother who, at 10:00 P.M., learns from her third-grader that she's expected to provide a snack for tomorrow's Halloween party.

1   cup popcorn (or Cracker Jacks)
½   cup candy corn
½   cup small marshmallows
½   cup black jelly beans

Mix all ingredients together in a colorful bowl.
Makes 8 servings.

Sugar Snakes in Graveyard Dust

Be sure to have plenty of napkins around for these "dusty" cookies! We can attribute this recipe to my older son, who makes strange things in the kitchen no matter what time of the year it is. His concoctions have become quite famous and often turn out to be pretty tasty. Because of the honey and sugar mixture, you can't prepare these too far in advance, as the honey and sugar seep into the cookie. Also, my son has also been known to use various holiday sprinkles (found in the baking section of the grocery store) for that added artistic touch.

2 tubes cookie dough (in the grocery store's dairy section)
   Chocolate chips
½ cup honey
2 tablespoons sugar
2 tablespoons cinnamon
   Confectioners' sugar

Separate dough into golfball-sized pieces, then separate each piece into four small balls. (Flour your fingers to keep the dough from sticking to them.) Roll out the balls in your hands into snakelike shapes. Place snakes one inch apart on cookie sheet. Bake at 350 degrees until snakes turn light brown. Remove from cookie sheets. When cookies are slightly warm to the touch, use chocolate chip pieces for the eyes. Allow to cool completely. Mix honey, sugar, and cinnamon in a small bowl and drizzle over cooled snakes right before serving. Sprinkle with confectioners' sugar (call it graveyard dust).

Oranges and Peppermint Sticks

This is an on-the-spot treat, and should not be prepared in advance.

- 1   orange for each guest
- 1   peppermint stick for each guest
- 1   apple corer

Roll the orange in your hands to make the insides nice and juicy. Use the apple corer to cut about ¾ of the way into the core of the orange. Place the peppermint stick in the hole, and use it as a straw.

Notes

1. Use *Cunningham's Encyclopedia of Magickal Herbs* by Scott Cunningham (Llewellyn, 1985).
2. Vesta is the fire goddess of hearth and home.
3. W. C. Hazlitt, *Dictionary of Faiths & Folklore Beliefs, Superstitions and Popular Customs*, Reeves and Turner, 1905, page 299.
4. Francis X. Weiser, *The Holyday Book*, Harcourt, 1956.

chapter
6

HALLOWEEN MAGICK

*May every trick
That you try to-night
Foretell a future
Of true delight.*
HALLOWEEN GREETINGS

—FROM AN EARLY NINETEENTH-CENTURY
HALLOWEEN POSTCARD

This chapter contains a compendium of enjoyable Halloween magick that you can try, designed and tested by myself and the members of the Black Forest Clan. Magick is defined as the art and science of changing circumstances to conform to your will—and, like any other skill, the more you work magick, the better you will become. Anyone can perform real magick, as long as you believe.

Love Apple Lights

You can tailor the apple spell for prosperity, protection, or spiritual prayer—or you can simply use the apple candles to decorate the table at your next Halloween party.

- 1   fresh apple, as large and glossy as you can find
      An apple corer (sold in local grocery or kitchen supply stores)
- 1   white taper candle

At fifteen minutes before midnight on Halloween Eve, hold the apple in your hands and ask Spirit to bless the fruit. Hum to yourself, thinking of bringing love into your life (but don't think of a specific person—that's a no-no). Continue to hum until the apple gets warm in your hands. Insert the apple corer into the stem of the apple and take out the core. Make sure not to make the hole bigger than the circumference of the candle. Hold the candle in your hands and hum again, thinking of bringing love toward you until, like the apple, the candle gets warm in your hands. Put the candle in the apple, and say:

> *Great Mother Goddess*
> *Sweet, divine*
> *Bring love to this heart of mine.*

Allow the candle to burn until it goes out, but keep a watchful eye on the apple to be sure no accidents happen.

The Love Apple Potion

Whip up some Halloween allure with this little potion. To add an extra little boost to this alluring potion, wrap the candle end in the red napkin and carry with you so you can be the most alluring person at that special Halloween party!

7   apple seeds
    Mortar and pestle
1   red candle
    Spring water
1   favorite clean decorative glass, chalice, or cup
1   square red cloth (a red napkin works well)
    Cheesecloth or a coffee filter

On a piece of paper, determine what love is to you. Double-check what you have written to be sure that you have not written words that would be against another's free will. If you have, please change the wording. Do not list any person by name. Warning: Your spell will backfire if you don't follow the rule of free will.

The day before Halloween Eve, crush the apple seeds into a fine powder using the mortar and pestle, chanting the following:

Love, love, love, love

All I want to be is loved.

Hold the red candle in your hand and think about giving and receiving love in your life. Concentrate for a minute or two, then light the candle, saying:

I invoke Venus, lady of love

I invoke Cupid, man of love

I invoke Aphrodite, lady of love

I invoke Spirit for universal love.

So mote it be.

Pass the mortar over the candle flame, saying:

I cleanse and consecrate this powder in the name of Spirit.

So mote it be.

Pour the spring water into a favorite clean decorative glass. Pour the powder into the cup, envisioning love and respect coming toward you from everyone in the universe. As you stare at the liquid, envision a blue flame of loving energy hovering over the cup, and then descending into the cup, infusing the liquid with universal love. Seal the energy over the cup with an equal-armed cross in the air.

Cover the cup with the red cloth. Let the powder steep for twelve hours. Let the candle burn until you have one inch left.

On Halloween, remove the red cloth from the top of the cup. Set the cloth aside. Strain through cheesecloth or a coffee filter.

Add potion to your favorite perfume, or use alone. Dab at pulse points on neck, wrists, and behind knees. Imagine yourself surrounded by universal love. Sprinkle a little of the potion on your Halloween costume.

Healing Love Pumpkin

To send healing love to someone over Samhain, try this little spell.

- 1   small pumpkin, hollowed
- 1   small piece white parchment
- 1   red pen
- 3   red roses
- 3   drops rose oil
- 1   green candle
- 1   green ribbon

On Samhain, cut off the top of the pumpkin. Hollow out the pumpkin and save the top. Write the person's name on the piece of parchment paper with the red pen. Roll up into a little tube. Place the tube at the bottom of the pumpkin. Fill the pumpkin with the rose petals, and add the rose oil.

Hold the green candle in your hands and say:

Samhain night, holy night,

send loving energy from the dawn of tomorrow

To the sunset of forever.

So mote it be.

Light the green candle and wave it around the pumpkin in a clockwise direction seven times, repeating the charm. Set the candle behind the pumpkin.

Hold your hands over the pumpkin and repeat the above charm until your hands get warm (or tingle) and you feel good inside. (**Note:** You can also perform this spell with an apple on any full moon for the same purpose.) Place the top on the pumpkin, then tie the green ribbon around the stem with the intention of sealing the spell.

Leave the candle burning until it is gone. You can also turn this spell into a seven-day ritual, beginning the evening of the full moon and continuing for six more days, lighting the candle for seven minutes every evening and allowing the remainder of the candle to burn on the night of the full moon.

Bury the pumpkin seven days after you perform the spell, or give your friend the pumpkin as a get-well Halloween gift.

Passion Pumpkin Dinner

Plan a romantic evening around a passion pumpkin. Prepare before your date arrives.

 1 large pumpkin
   Heart cookie cutter
   Red felt-tipped pen
   Pumpkin cutting tools (the kind you can buy at the grocery store)
   Patchouli oil
   Take-out Italian or Chinese food
   Pink tablecloth
 1 red votive candle and holder
   Red roses and white baby's breath (if you don't live on a rose budget,
     use red and white carnations)
   Rose petals
 2 red taper candles

Hollow out the pumpkin. Use the cookie cutter and the red pen to trace hearts all over the pumpkin. Use the pumpkin cutting tools to cut out the hearts. Wrap the hearts in cellophane and put them in the refrigerator. Coat the inside of the pumpkin lightly with patchouli oil. One hour before your date arrives, pick up the take-out food (or better yet, have it delivered if you can). Keep the food warm in the oven.

Set the table with the pink tablecloth, putting the pumpkin in the center. Put the rose petals in the pumpkin holder, then drop in the votive, or scatter rose petals on a white linen napkin that covers your lover's plate. Light the votive candle and drop both the votive and holder into the pumpkin. Put patchouli oil lightly on the back of the pumpkin hearts from the refrigerator. Put the carnations or roses around the base of the pumpkin, arranged with the pumpkin hearts. Oil the candles lightly with patchouli oil. Set them on either side of the pumpkin. Hold your hands over the centerpiece, and say:

Heart divine and flowers of love

Pumpkin power and Spirit above

Turn and swirl

Turn and swirl

Turn and swirl

Bring me happiness, joy, and love.

Hold your hands over the centerpiece until your palms tingle or grow warm and you feel good inside. Light the red candles, repeating the words "divine union." The rest, of course, is up to the two of you.

Pumpkin Abundance Lights

These are great for magickal party favors and will cost you very little.

- 6   miniature pumpkins
- 6   tea lights
-    Knife or pumpkin carving tools

Cut off the tops of the little pumpkins and clean them out (save those seeds!). Cut happy faces into the pumpkins. Insert tea lights. Hold your hands over the pumpkins and chant:

Gold and silver

Coins galore

All are coming

To your door.[1]

Keeps your hands over the pumpkins until your palms tingle or grow warm. Give them to your friends with a smile, and repeat the spell to them. Tell them to light the candle in the pumpkin at midnight on Halloween to activate the spell.

Magick Harvest Seed Picture

Here's a great harvest project for the kids. It'll keep them busy for hours and help them to learn how to focus on a specific goal.

Orange cardboard
Pencil
School glue
An old paint brush
Dried seeds and beans in different colors:
  Pumpkin (abundance)
  Corn (protection and luck)
  Beans (charming)
  Mustard (fertility)
  Apple (love)
  Peas (money)
  Sunflower (wishes and wisdom)

On the first day of October, draw a picture of your goal on the cardboard with the pencil.

Brush the glue onto one section of the picture. Place the seeds in any pattern on that section, as your desire here is more important than the pattern itself, though you could use magickal sigils if you so desired. Think about your goal and bringing it to fruition.

Each day complete another section of the picture, thinking about bringing the goal to fruition.

On Halloween Eve, hold your hands over the completed picture and ask Spirit help you to obtain your goal. Hold your hands over the picture until your palms tingle or become warm.

Hang the picture where you can see it every day. As long as you feel positive about the goal, keep the picture out. If you feel negative, like it isn't coming fast enough, put the picture away. Every time you look at the picture, ask Spirit help you manifest your goal.

When your goal has come to fruition, thank Spirit and burn the picture.

Morgana's Blessing Incense

This wonderful incense comes from Morgana, of Morgana's Chamber in New York City. You can use this recipe to enhance any magickal working or ceremony. Works well in sachet magick as well.

- ¼ cup sea salt (cleansing)
- 1 tablespoon finely powdered cinnamon (raises spiritual vibrations)
- ½ tablespoon finely powdered benzoin resin (purification)
- 1 teaspoon finely powdered dragon's blood resin (adds power)
- 1 teaspoon dark musk oil (passion)
- 1 teaspoon slightly crushed lavender buds (love)
- 1 teaspoon finely crushed rose petals (love)

Put sea salt in a glass bowl. Add ingredients, one at a time, mixing well after each addition. Add small amounts to charcoal and burn. Keep extra incense in a tightly covered jar.

Jack-o'-Lantern Protection Totem

We've used this great idea for the last several years at our house (ever since someone ran away with a rocking chair and scarecrow on Mischief Night). These carved pumpkins of your design will keep those drifting fingers away from your Halloween decorations!

3–5 pumpkins of various sizes with flat bottoms (be careful that your pumpkin isn't overripe)

Pumpkin cutting tools

A design for each pumpkin (except the base pumpkin)

A metal fence post or broom handle

1 (5-pound) bag kitty litter

1 ounce angelica or other herb known for its folklore protection properties

Cut the top off of each pumpkin and scoop out the insides. Save the seeds for your Halloween party, pumpkin seed divination (page 81), toasted pumpkin seeds (page 109), the magick harvest seed picture (page 132), or the the prosperity pumpkin spell (page 157).

Cut a hole in the bottom of each pumpkin the same size as the pole or broomstick.

Carve the designs you have chosen on each pumpkin. As you carve, think about scaring away negative energies, mean people, and other things that go bump in the night. Do not carve the base pumpkin.

Drive the metal fence post or broom handle down into the ground. Slide the base pumpkin down the post. Empty the bag of kitty litter into the base pumpkin. Hold the angelica in your hands and empower for protection and blessings. Sprinkle the angelica on top of the kitty litter.

Add the next smallest pumpkin. Continue in this order, from largest (base) to smallest. You may have to trim the pumpkins so that they set securely.

Stand back from the pumpkin totem, hold your hands over your creation, and ask Spirit to bless your totem and protect your home.

You can add nonflammable pumpkin lights on Halloween Eve or even attach electric Halloween blinking lights if your totem is near an outlet. Surround with cornstalks for an extraspecial effect!

When it is time to tear the pumpkin totem down, be sure to once again hold your hands over the totem and thank Spirit for the protective energies. Imagine that energy seeping out from the pumpkins and into the ground. Take apart the totem and dispose.

If you don't feel like carving all those faces, use the same idea to make a scarecrow. Stack pumpkins and carve only the head. Glue some straw to the pumpkin head and add an old hat!

Halloween Reversing Negativity

If you have been experiencing a lot of negativity around your house (frequent arguments, depression, general unhappiness, and so on), you might want to try this spell.

1   medium-sized pumpkin
    A VERY scary pumpkin face that you have designed yourself
    Pumpkin carving tools
1   white votive candle
    A small, heat-resistant glass plate that will fit inside the pumpkin
7   black pillar candles
1   black votive candle

The day before Samhain, carve your scary face in the pumpkin while humming:

Scary face and monster wiles

Goblin glint and Witches' smiles

Repel the evil with pumpkin eyes.

Candles black and orange sun

Send all evil on the run!

Hold the white votive candle in your hands, saying:

I cleanse and consecrate you

In the name of Spirit.

Put the white candle on the plate, and put the plate in the pumpkin. Do not put the top on the pumpkin. Burn the white candle for one full evening in the pumpkin. On Samhain Eve, hold each black pillar candle and the black votive candle (one at a time) in your hands and say the same verse again:

Scary face and monster wiles

Goblin glint and Witches' smiles

Repel the evil with pumpkin eyes.

Candles black and orange sun

Send all evil on the run!

Set the pillar candles around the pumpkin in a circle. Replace the white candle in the pumpkin with the black votive candle.

Light each pillar candle, saying the same verse. Light the black votive candle in the pumpkin (be very careful not to burn yourself). Hold your hands over the pumpkin (but not so close that you burn your arms on the pillar candles) and continue to chant the verse until your hands grow hot or tingle, and you feel good inside. Let the candles burn until 3:00 A.M. Do not leave candles unattended. You can use the pillar candles for future repelling negativity spells. Set the pumpkin outside, facing away from the house, to continue to act as a negativity repellent. Allow to rot (if you can).

Halloween Defense Spell

If you know someone has purposefully set out to hurt you, then you might wish to try your hand at this defense spell. Be careful, though, because you could be subconsciously attacking yourself. Take a good, hard look at the situation to determine if you may be the cause. You might be reaping the rewards of your own actions. If this is the case, rather than casting a spell, begin working toward changing your lifestyle and attitude.

A piece of orange construction paper
A black felt-tipped pen
1 black candle
2 pieces straw, tied together like an equal-armed cross with black thread
Morgana's incense (page 133) or sandlewood incense

On the Saturday closest to Halloween, gather the above supplies. Cut the orange paper in the shape of a pumpkin. On the paper, draw the figure of the person who is attacking you, then write their name underneath. (Artistic talent is not an issue.) If you don't know who is causing you so much difficulty, then write "Whoever is attacking me" on the orange pumpkin.

Hold the black candle in your hand and think about negativity moving away from you. Take a minute or two to concentrate. Say:

> *In the name of Our Mother*
>
> *Whose delicate hand can raise the seas to a raging surf*
>
> *Whose brilliant eyes can see the truth in all that is*
>
> *Whose source of strength can match that of a thousand lions*
>
> *I call thee forth to turn the tides of this negative tempest*
>
> *To protect and heal the victim*
>
> *To send back the evil experienced here.*
>
> *Come, O Great Mother*
>
> *And hear the petition of the faithful.*

Hold the pumpkin paper over the flame (do not burn the paper) and say the attacker's name aloud. Use your finger to write the person's name in the air above the candle. Do this three times.

Burn the cross and the paper in a fire-safe dish, and say:

> *Three angels came from the north*
>
> *Bringing water and fire.*
>
> *Three blows hast the enemy dealt me*
>
> *By head, by heart, by tongue.*
>
> *The first angel said, "These same blows I return."*
>
> *The second angel said, "This is the reward you have earned."*
>
> *The third angel said, "You reap what you sow."*
>
> *By fire and water, earth and air*
>
> *The angels return the evil there.*

Draw a upright star in the air over the candle. This is called banishing.

Mix up a batch of Morgana's incense (or use prepackaged sandlewood incense). Light the incense and walk around your house, saying:

> *I banish all negativity resting here.*
>
> *I cleanse this area in the name of the Great Mother.*
>
> *So mote it be.*

Give the ashes to the winds. Allow the candle to burn until nothing is left. If the candle end should remain, bury the end off your property or dispose in a living body of water.

The Pumpkin Separation Spell

Unfortunately, we all get into predicaments in which we feel trapped. This pumpkin spell has never failed us.

- 2 miniature pumpkins
  A black felt-tipped pen
- ⅛ teaspoon black pepper
- ⅛ teaspoon red pepper
- ⅛ teaspoon salt
- 14 tea candles

Seven days before Samhain, hollow out both pumpkins. Write your name on the bottom of one pumpkin and the situation (or person) you wish to be removed from on the bottom of the other pumpkin. Sprinkle the two peppers and salt in the bottom of the pumpkin of the other person or situation. Vent both pumpkins with a small carved design (your choice). Set the tops of the pumpkins in an open plastic bag in your refrigerator.

Set the pumpkins three inches apart on a table where they will not be disturbed. Hold your hands over the pumpkins, and say:

> *Pumpkin light, Witches' fright*
>
> *Send **(name the situation or person)** away this night.*

Keep repeating the charm until the palms of your hands become warm or tingle. Put a tea candle in each pumpkin and light them. (Don't burn yourself.) Let burn for one hour. Do not leave unattended.

Each evening, change the candles, move the pumpkins another inch apart, and repeat the charm. On Samhain Eve, repeat the spell at midnight. Let candles burn until 3:00 A.M. Do not leave candles unattended. Put out the candles. Close up both pumpkins with their respective lids. Bury one pumpkin on one side of a river, creek, or railroad crossing (please do not go on the tracks). Bury the other pumpkin on the other side of the creek, river, or railroad crossing. If you can't bury them, then throw the pumpkins into a living body of water (not near each other).

Do not throw the spent candles in the water. You can throw them in a dumpster away from your house.

Note: If something strange happens with the pumpkins that would cut your spell short (like if the pumpkin collapses), don't worry about it. This means that the spell has been activated and you don't need to continue. Dispose of both pumpkins in the manner listed above. When my daughter does this spell, invariably one or the other pumpkins disintegrates in less than two days (which is why I warn you not to leave the little pumpkins unattended).

Samhain Protection Powder

Powders, for whatever reason, carry an association with Voodoo practitioners, but I've found them used extensively in early American Witchcraft by Pow-Wow Doctors/Artists. In Pennsylvania and West Virginia, practitioners sometimes used corn meal as a base ingredient to hide the essence of the powder. Where Voodoo practitioners want you to know they are cooking magick, Pow-Wow Doctors/Artists didn't want you to find out.

The simple act of making a powder won't automatically pull the magickal essence into the mixture. Just as you activate other magickal tools, you must activate the powder through some sort of spellworking, chant or whispering magick, or ritual. Take into consideration the elements you used to create your powder. Earth and air are always present in a magickal powder, but if you add it to a liquid, then the water element gets equal billing. If you plan to burn the powder, then you need to set the magickal stage for the fire element as well.

This powder is designed to work on Halloween Eve and can be used in spellwork or alone. You will need equal parts of the following:

> Chili powder (protection and exorcism)
> Black pepper (protection and exorcism)
> Angelica (protection and exorcism)
> Rosemary (protection)
> Basil (protection)
> Pumpkin spice (protection)
> Cloves (protection)
> Black talc, optional

This powder is best made on Saturday during a full moon. Use a mortar and pestle to slowly grind ingredients into a fine powder. You can add orris root as a preservative if you plan to make a large batch to give some to your friends. Hum the word "protection" as you mix the powder. Store in a dry place until Halloween Eve.

At midnight on Halloween Eve, hold a black candle in your hands and ask Spirit to move all negativity away from you, from the present and throughout the coming year. Light the candle. Put the powder into a clean bowl. Hold your hands over the powder, and say:

> *Witches' lair and spirit-wolf night*
> *Ancient Ones bring second sight*
> *Blood and bones of those before*
> *Help me with this little chore.*
>
> *Herbs and talc and natural things*
> *At my bidding, safety bring.*
> *North for earth, and east for air*
> *I summon Spirit to help me here.*

Sprinkle some of the powder around the black candle. Allow the candle to burn completely. Bury the candle end off your property. As long as the powder lasts, you can sprinkle it in the corners of a room to overcome feelings of irritation and anger (even at the office). The mixture helps to avert future fights and will cleanse the mind of all evil thoughts, and helps clear the head when you are experiencing negative emotions.

Porch Protection Turnips

If you have a front porch, these lanterns will shine protective light on your home Halloween Eve or Trick-or-Treating Night.

13   large turnips
     A sharp paring knife
13   tealight candles
     A hand drill
     Picture-hanging wire
     A black felt-tipped pen

Cut off the tops of the turnips. Discard tops. Hollow out enough of the turnip to drop in the tealight candle and protect the flame from the wind. With the hand drill, drill a hole on each side of the turnip an inch or so from the top (so you're cutting into the hollowed-out section), so the wire can loop through the hole. Secure, then loop through the opposite hole. Secure and cut wire. This will serve as the handle or hanger for your turnip. You can make the wire as long as you desire. Decorate the white area of the turnip with magickal symbols of protection, such as the rune Algiz (ᛉ). Hold your hands over the finished project, and say:

> *From dusk till dawn*
>
> *Ancient protection I call hither*
>
> *Blessings of those beyond the veil.*

Hold your hands over the turnips until your palms grow warm or tingle and you feel good inside. When you are ready to use the turnips, light the candles, saying:

> *Blessings of Vesta upon this house.*

Hang outside (or inside). Do not leave unattended. Bury on your property seven days after Samhain to continue the magickal protection of your property.

Autumn Conjuration

This spell requires a trip to the park or a walk in the woods. Take a plastic bag and collect all the large, beautiful leaves you can find (not the dry, crumbly ones). When you get home, you will need the following:

> An iron
> Glue

Spread the leaves on a table. Hold your hands over the leaves, and say:

> *My life is filled with abundance*
>
> *And all my needs are met—and more.*

Keep repeating this chant until your hands grow warm. Finish by saying:

> *Autumn harvest, bring to me*
>
> *Abundance, joy, and laughter.*
>
> *So mote it be.*

Put the iron on the lowest setting and smooth out the leaves.

Glue the leaves together in circles or ovals to create autumn place mats. If you are very industrious and would like to make an altar cloth out of the leaves, glue the leaves together in squares, then press the squares on fusible webbing, following the instructions on the package. One warning, however: These leaves are flammable, therefore do not burn candles directly on them.

Another variation of this spell requires:

> 1 block paraffin
> Colorful leaves you have collected
> An old pot that you will never use again
> A large clear brandy snifter or other glass bowl

Follow the same procedures of empowerment with the leaves as listed above. Iron the leaves to flatten them. Heat the paraffin over low heat on the stove. When the paraffin has completely melted, dip the leaves by their stems into the pot, covering them with paraffin, then lift the leaves out, allowing excess wax to dribble back in the pot and the wax to harden on the leaf. When the wax is sufficiently cool, place the leaf carefully on a hard, smooth surface. Allow to dry thoroughly. When the leaves are totally dry, arrange in the snifter or bowl. They will last several months.

Halloween Pleasant Dream Sachets

These dream sachets are a wonderful idea for Halloween party favors, however, you must plan ahead and make them a few weeks before your Halloween party, depending on the moon phase you wish to use (full moon for protection, new moon for pleasant beginnings).

Halloween-design material to make small sachet bags (or you can buy premade sachet bags from a craft store and decorate)
Orange and black ribbons
4　tablespoons dried lavender buds (love, protection, restful sleep)
20　whole cloves (love and protection)
4　tablespoons dried rosemary (protection and love)
½　teaspoon dried orange peel (love)
1　sunflower seed for each sachet (wisdom)

Mix lavender, cloves, rosemary, and orange peel together in a small bowl. Hold your hands over the bowl of herbs and say:

From mother moon and father sun

From autumn breezes carrying angel prayers

I empower these herbs to bring protection and love

To whoever holds them between clasped hands

And prays for restful sleep.

Hold your hands over the herbs until your hands grow warm. Fill the sachet bags, then empower the sunflower seeds, saying:

From mother moon and father sun

From autumn breezes carrying angel prayers

I empower these herbs to bring protection and love

To whoever holds them between clasped hands

And prays for restful sleep.

Tie up sachets, reaffirming with each sachet:

From mother moon and father sun

From autumn breezes carrying angel prayers

I empower these herbs to bring protection and love

To whoever holds them between clasped hands

And prays for restful sleep.

This recipe will make approximately 7 to 10 small sachets.

Samhain House Blessing Potpourri

You should make this mixture approximately six weeks before your Samhain celebration on a full moon.

- 4   cups dried rose and other flowers of your choice (love)
- 1   cup dried lemon verbena leaves (purification and joy)
- 1   cup dried lavender buds (protection and love)
- 1   tablespoon dried rosemary (protection and love)
- 1   tablespoon basil (protection and love)
- 1   tablespoon marjoram (protection and love)
- 2   tablespoons cloves (protection)
- 2   tablespoons cinnamon (protection, love, and psychic powers)
- 2   tablespoons nutmeg (health)
- 1   vanilla bean, crushed (love)
- 1   tablespoon grated orange rind (love)
- 1   tablespoon grated lemon rind (protection)
- 2   tablespoons orris root (this is a preservative as well as a psychic correspondence)
- 6   drops lavender oil

Place the first ingredient on the list in a very large bowl. Hold your hands over the ingredient and begin humming the words "love" and "protection." Repeat until your hands grow warm. Add each ingredient in the same way, mixing lightly with your hands while chanting/humming. Add lavender oil last. Seal mixture in a jar and place in a warm, dry place (not too warm). Shake the jar each day, humming the words "love" and "protection." This mixture needs six weeks to cure, so remember to start early. The night of your Samhain party, open the jar and pour contents into a pretty bowl. Carry the bowl around the entire house, humming the words "love" and "protection." Ring a bell in every room to clear out any remaining negative influences. Leave the bowl in the room with the most traffic. If you are having a Halloween party or Samhain ritual, you could use the potpourri as a centerpiece. Discard around your house before Yule, then make a new batch for the Yule season.

Halloween Wish Candle

Wishes can come true and this simple little spell is designed to assist you in manifesting your wishes. Be careful, though—you may get what you wish for, so wish wisely!

1 (8-inch) candle in a glass container
Tissue paper in different colors
Scissors
Reversible collage glue

Cut the tissue paper into Halloween shapes (cats, pumpkins, brooms, stars, moons, and so on). Coat the glass candle with the glue and lay the tissue paper shapes on the glue. Coat the tissue paper with another layer of glue. Let dry thoroughly.

Empower your candle by holding it in your hands and thinking of your wish. Say:

Creature of fire

Lend your will to my desire.

Hold the candle in your hands until your palms tingle or become warm. On Halloween Eve, light the candle. Let the candle go out naturally. Soak container in hot water to remove all wax. If your goal has not manifested by this time, draw a picture of your original wish and place it in the container. Hold your hands over the container, and say:

Creature of air

Lend your will to my desire.

Blow seven times into the container. Put the container in a safe place until your wish comes true. After your wish comes true, be sure to thank deity for making it happen.

Corn Husk Magick

Corn husks are the outer foliage that protect the ear of corn. You can buy already cleaned and bleached husks from hobby suppliers, or you can do this procedure yourself. The tradition of making corn husk dolls came from the Native American Indians. Today, in the Ozark Mountains of Missouri and the Southern Appalachians, corn-husk-crafted dolls remain part of the American culture.

There are lots of things you can do with corn husks, once you let your imagination take hold. To prepare corn husks, shuck the husks carefully, trying to not tear the leaves. You can cut off the base of the corn to make this an easier process, and peel from the top down. Spread on newspapers or paper towels and let dry in a warm place until shriveled and creamy in color. Depending on your spell, you can bleach the husks, as they tend to discolor. Place the husks in a bowl of water with ½ cup of household bleach and allow to sit for 15 minutes, or until discoloration has disappeared. Be careful, though, because if you let the husks sit in the bleach water too long, they will disintegrate. Rinse the husks in clear water. You can dye corn husks by using ordinary household dyes and following the directions on the dye package.

To create shapes with corn husks, work with them damp, using string tied to the center of the husks, then bend the tops over. You can design corn husk flowers or other unusual shapes, including a corn dolly, in this manner. (See page 149.)

If this technique takes too long for you, not to worry! Cut out a female shape or male shape from thin cardboard. Glue corn husk pieces to the cardboard. Trim. Empower the corn person with your desire. If you are working for someone who is ill, say his or her name three times, then say:

I forge a link between (person's name) *and this corn dolly.*
As the sun rises and sets each day until All Hallows Eve
You will get better and better.
Total good health will be yours.

Party guests can burn their wishes on Halloween Eve by writing, with a black marker, what they wish for on a piece of dry corn husk. Feed to the Samhain fires, saying:

Corn husk will give way to flame

The essence of the word remains

Fire destroy and fire create

Let what's written be my fate! [2]

The group can chant the word "change" while each person burns their corn husk.

Corn Husk Dolly

As we learned earlier in this book, the significance of the corn dolly is to bring health, wealth, and general prosperity to the land or property owner. Here are instructions on how you can make a small dolly for your home.

Dried corn husks

Straight pins

Ruler

Scissors

Button or carpet thread

Pipe cleaners or wire

White glue

Small styrofoam ball or wooden bead for head

Rubber band

Dip dried husks in warm water to make them pliable, about 15 minutes. Drain and wrap in a damp towel until ready to use. If you can't complete the doll in one sitting, you can redampen and finish later.

To make the head, take a corn husk piece (3 by 7 inches) and fold right over left. Insert a piece of wire in the styrofoam or wooden bead, cover with white glue, and place in the middle of the husk (the husk wraps right over left around the styrofoam). Tie tightly just above the bead, then bring the top of the husk down over the head and tie again at the neck. (see Illustration 1)

Illustration 1

Illustration 2

For the arms, put a 4½-inch length of wire along the grain of a strip of husk that is 5½ inches long and 3½ inches wide. Roll to form a tight cylinder. Trim the ends so that the total length is about 5 inches. Tie (or wire) each end at the wrists. (see Illustration 2)

Gather a 3-inch by 3½-inch piece of husk around one arm about ½ to ¾ inches above the wrist and tie securely, overlapping the ends. Pull this husk back toward the center to form a puffed sleeve and tie near the center. Repeat this process for

Illustration 4

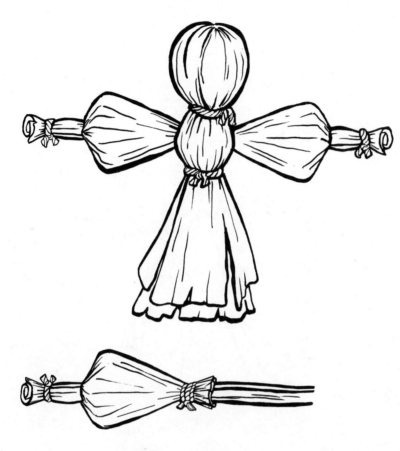

Illustration 3

the other arm. Insert the arms between the neck pieces and tie below the bust. (see Illustration 3)

Select two strips of dampened husk about 1½ inches to 2 inches wide and 5 inches long, and place them in front of and behind the head. Tie just above the arms and pull the back husk down to the waist. Lay a small piece of cotton at the bust, pull the front husk down, and tie front and back strips at the waist. (see Illustration 4)

Illustration 5

Illustration 6

For the bodice, lay two ⅝-inch by 5-inch strips to form an X across the bust. Bring these strips down and across behind the doll, and tie at the waist. (see Illustration 5)

Bend the arms up and lay a number of poorer quality husks around the body. Tie firmly at the waist, then pull the tops of the strips down to form the underskirt. Trim to ¼-inch shorter than the desired skirt length. Secure with a rubber band. (see Illustration 6)

Illustration 7

Illustration 8

Cut a strip for the apron and lay at the waist, extending upward. Choose 4 clean husks about 5 inches wide (use more if the strips are narrower) and place one in front, one in back, and two on the sides. Pull these layers down carefully, bringing the apron down last. Trim to desired length. Tie a narrow strip around the waist. (see Illustration 7)

Encircle skirt loosely with a rubber band to hold in place until the husks dry. Add hair, features, and accessories as desired. (see Illustration 8)

Halloween Charm Bags

Many magickal people make charm bags and employ them as talismans to attract positive energies. This little bag is carried on the person, either in a pocket or around the neck, until the desired outcome manifests. The bag and its contents help you to focus and, once empowered, aid in pulling the desired energies to you. Here are three Samhain recipes.

Charm Bag for Drawing Money

- 7 pumpkin seeds
- ¼ teaspoon dried, ground pumpkin rind
- ¼ teaspoon dried mint
- ¼ teaspoon cinnamon
- 1 silver coin
- 1 small orange flannel bag with 17-inch red ribbon
- Black felt pen

On the new moon before Halloween, mix herbal ingredients together. Hum:

East and west, south and north

Prosperity, I bring thee forth.

Draw a dollar sign on both sides of each pumpkin seed with the black felt pen. Add the pumpkin seeds to the mixture. Pour into orange bag. Hold the coin in your hands until it gets warm, humming the same chant. Put the coin in the bag and tie it up. On the following Thursday, hold the bag in your hands and repeat the chant until the bag becomes warm in your hands. Add seven knots to the ribbon around the bag: one for beginnings, two for money, three for abundance, four for stability, five for protection from blocks, six for luck, and the seventh knot to seal the spell. Put in a special place until Samhain. On Samhain, hold the bag in your hands over the need-fire and repeat the chant until the bag warms in your hands and you feel good inside.

Keep on your person or in your purse or wallet. Good for one full year. You can rework the spell on a new moon to keep the bag at its peak. Replace the following Samhain. This makes a very nice gift for that special friend in your life.

Charm Bag for Healing

3	pumpkin seeds
¼	teaspoon allspice
¼	teaspoon dried eucalyptus
¼	teaspoon dried, ground lime rind
¼	teaspoon dried, ground pumpkin rind
1	dried ivy leaf
	The sick person's name written on a small piece of paper
	Small green felt bag with 17-inch green ribbon

On the full moon before Halloween, mix herbs together, saying:

Spice and rind, leaf and love

Bring Spirit healing from above.

Hold your hands over the mixture, saying the same chant, until the palms of your hands get warm or tingle. Add the herbs and the person's name written on a small piece of paper to the charm bag. Tie the bag. Repeat the chant. On the following Sunday, add five knots: one for healing, two for love, three for Spirit, four for stability, and five to seal the spell. Hold the bag in your hands and repeat the chant until the bag grows warm in your hands. On Samhain, hold the bag over the need-fire and repeat the chant again until the bag grows warm in your hands and you feel good inside. Give the bag to the ailing person as a Samhain gift. Tell him or her to carry the bag with them until they get better.

Charm Bag for Luck

1 small guardian angel pin or Miraculous Medal medallion
7 small white feathers
1 small piece white cotton
¼ teaspoon rose petals
¼ teaspoon dried, ground pumpkin rind
¼ teaspoon dried, ground orange peel
¼ teaspoon dried, crushed straw
7 pumpkin seeds
Small orange felt bag with 17-inch orange ribbon

On the new moon before Samhain, mix the herbs together in a bowl, saying:

Guardian angel, peace and love
Bring me luck on wings of dove.

Hold your hands over the mixture and say the same chant until your palms grow warm or tingle. Hold the medallion or pin in your hand and repeat the chant. Pour the mixture in the bag. Add medallion. Tie the bag with the orange ribbon. Repeat the chant, holding the bag in your hands until the bag grows warm. On the first Thursday after the new moon, hold the bag in your hands and repeat the chant until the bag grows warm. Tie nine knots in the ribbon: one for beginnings, two for partnership with your guardian angel, three for luck, four for stability, five for removal of all blocks, six for love, seven for change to better circumstances, eight for swift luck. and nine to seal the spell. On Samhain, hold the bag over the need-fire and repeat the chant once again, until the bag grows warm in your hands and you feel good inside. Keep the bag with you. Should last one year if you remember to renew the bag every new moon. Make a new bag the following Samhain.

Prosperity Pumpkin Spell

If you need to harvest a little money this Samhain season, try this spell.

1   small (not miniature)-sized pumpkin
     The amount of money that you need, written on a piece of plain
        white paper in green ink (if you don't know how much you need,
        give a rough figure, but don't make the request outrageous—the
        universe works on our needs, not necessarily on our wants)
1   bag fresh dirt
7   dimes
7   pumpkin seeds from this pumpkin
7   ounces rain water or water from a stream (no tap or bottled water)
     Pencil
     Lodestone, optional

Cut the top of the pumpkin off in a scallop design (to aid in the flow of money to you). Clean out the pumpkin. (Save the seeds for other magickal work.) Remember to keep seven seeds for this spell. Place the pumpkin in the refrigerator until Halloween Eve.

One-half hour before Halloween Eve (not after), bring out the pumpkin, the piece of paper with the dollar amount you need written on it, the dirt, dimes, seeds, and the water. Place the paper in the bottom of the pumpkin. Pour in the dirt. With the end of a pencil, make seven holes in the dirt in a circular pattern (keep the holes at least one inch apart). Hold the first dime in your hand and think about the amount of money you need. (Important: do not think negative thoughts about the money you need, no matter how desperate you are.) Keep the dime in your hand until it grows warm and you feel good inside. With the pencil, push the first dime in the hole that coincides with 12 o'clock. Follow the same procedure, going clockwise, with the other six dimes. (If you happen to have a lodestone hanging around, bury it in the middle of the dirt.)

Now, starting at 12 o'clock and going clockwise, pour 1 ounce of water into each hole. Think of your prosperity as you pour the water into each hole. When you are finished, hold your hands over the pumpkin and say:

One dime for beginnings

One dime for drawing

One dime for growth

One dime for stability

One dime for banishing negativity

One dime for luck

One dime to seal the spell.

So mote it be!

Bury the pumpkin outside on your property the following night one-half hour before midnight (no later).

Solitary Harvest Moon Ritual

I designed this harvest ritual for an individual of any faith—just replace the listed deity with the one you worship. There is no reason on this planet why you cannot thank deity for the abundance you have received in the past year and request additional love, fruitful harvests, and protection for the coming year.

- 1   straw bale
- 1   large, flat stone
- 2   orange pillar candles (Spirit candles)
-     A plate with one slice of homemade bread
- 1   cup filled with cider
-     A white cloth (the size of a white linen napkin)
- 1   small charcoal incense tab
-     Incense burner
-     Morgana's blessing incense (page 133)
-     Symbol of your deity (statue, picture, drawing, and so on)
-     Fruits of the local harvest

    Offerings for the quarters:
        A bowl of flowers for the north
        A bowl of water for the west
        A bowl of small gourds and pumpkins for the east
        A bowl of corn or Indian corn for the south
    Harvest decorations of your choice

1   pledge (not too difficult) written on a piece of paper (for example: "I will be more loving to others in the coming year")

1   bowl

One hour before sunset on Samhain Eve (or another night during the month of October if you like), set up the straw bale outside (straw bales tend to leak bits of straw in case you have a neat fetish). Be sure to place it so that you will be facing the sunset. Place the flat stone on top of the bale. Put the two pillar candles on the stone near its farthest edge from you. Place the bread and cider to the left of the stone, and cover with a white cloth. Place the charcoal in an incense burner on the right side of the stone. Add incense. Place your statue or picture between the candles. Place the fruits of the local harvest in the center of the stone. Put the decorations at their appropriate compass points: flowers at the north, water at the west, and so on, around you. Now add the harvest decorations, the pledge, and the bowl either on the bale or directly below it, within easy reach.

Take a shower or bath and ask Spirit to cleanse your body. (Don't take too long, you don't want to miss the sunset.)

When you are ready to begin the ritual, hold your hands over the straw bale and ask deity to bless the items on the straw and to bless the room (or out-of-doors area where you are standing). Close your eyes and allow deity to be with you—nothing will grab you or hurt you. You aren't calling anything but the god or goddess you believe in.

Light the Spirit candles, and say:

I light these candles in the name of Spirit

(or in the names of the Lord and Lady, or whomever you desire).

Take a few moments to contemplate those things in your life this year that have turned out well for you. No action or issue is too small. After each thought, thank Spirit for that opportunity and watch the sun set. Enjoy the beautiful colors, the smell of autumn, the gift that you are alive.

Hold your hands over the harvest items on the straw bale and thank deity for the harvests you have reaped this year. Ask for continued good will and fruitfulness in your life for the coming year.

Hold your hands over the cider, and say:

From the sun to the root

From the root to the vine

From the vine to the berry

I bless this cider in the name of (name your deity here).

May I never thirst.

Drink from the glass. Pour the contents onto the ground (or into a bowl you have placed on the floor by the straw), and say:

In offering to (name deity).

Hold your hands over the bread, and say:

From the moon to the root

From the root to the stalk

From the stalk to wheat

I bless this bread in the name of (name your deity here).

May I never hunger.

Eat a portion of the bread. Drop the remaining bread onto the ground (or into the bowl with cider), and say:

In offering to (name deity).

As you watch the sun set, say your favorite prayer, sing a song, and become one with the universe. When the sun sets, once again thank deity for your gifts and close your eyes. Thank deity for being with you today.

The ritual is finished. You can take the straw bale apart and use it to cover some of your favorite perennials in your garden or use it on your mulch pile.

Summary

Magick is the art and science of using your focus and universal energies to change your circumstances for the better. If you found this chapter interesting, and would like to delve further into either the practice of Wicca or general magickal applications, please review the suggested reading list on the next page.

Notes

1. Written by Breid FoxSong, New York.
2. Written by Jack Veasey.

Suggested Reading List

Beginning Wicca

To Ride A Silver Broomstick: New Generation WitchCraft by Silver RavenWolf (Llewellyn, 1993). A beginner's guide to Wicca.

Teen Witch: Wicca for a New Generation by Silver RavenWolf (Llewellyn, 1998). Wicca for ages 13 through 18.

Wicca: A Guide for the Solitary Practitioner by Scott Cunningham (Llewellyn, 1988).

The Truth About Witchcraft Today by Scott Cunningham (Llewellyn, 1988).

Folk Magick

American Folk Magick by Silver RavenWolf (Llewellyn, 1995).

Mountain Magick by Edain McCoy (Llewellyn, 1997).

General Magick

Angels: Companions in Magick by Silver RavenWolf (Llewellyn, 1996).

Modern Magick by Donald Michael Kraig (Llewellyn, 1988).

Tarot Spells by Janine Renee (Llewellyn, 1990).

Witches Runes by Nigel Jackson and Silver RavenWolf (Llewellyn, 1996). A book and card deck.

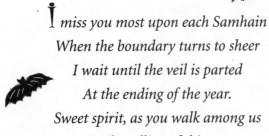

chapter 7

HALLOWEEN: A TIME TO HONOR THE DEAD

I miss you most upon each Samhain
When the boundary turns to sheer
I wait until the veil is parted
At the ending of the year.
Sweet spirit, as you walk among us
At the tolling of this eve
I see your face beyond the sunset
And hear your voice upon the breeze.

In the glowing of the candle,
From the shadow on the wall
I watch for you in every movement
And hear your footsteps in the hall.
Can you sit and spend the evening
As the portal opens wide?
Ancestral dead, I bid you welcome,
Most recent dead, I pray, abide.

When you come I sense your presence
I put my hand out in the air
A moment, then, we stand united
Palm to palm while waiting there.
I miss you most upon each Samhain
When the boundary turns to sheer
We share these hours until the dawning
Then bid farewell until next year.

— © 1988 DAVID O. NORRIS,
"UPON EACH SAMHAIN"

When I was seventeen, my mother died of a fast-killing cancer. It was through her journey to the Other Side that I became involved in the study of religion and the magickal arts. There is nothing more serious in life than learning to deal with the death of a loved one. I have also learned that no one religion totally encompasses God, nor is there a single religion that has all the answers. We need to choose what works for us, and decide what practices allow us to feel that special closeness with deity.

With the American need to isolate ourselves from others, we have also frozen ourselves in a religious time warp. What worked for us and the community in 1958 or 1972 may not help us now, especially when dealing with the painful issue of death. We need to seek, and to find, valid practices that will help us understand and deal with death in a positive way.

Talking to the Dead

There is nothing wrong with going into a room by yourself, or taking a walk in the cemetery, or sitting in a favorite nature spot and talking aloud to a dead loved one. You are not crazy. You are not stupid. You are not weak. You are human. Did you know that over sixty percent of widows and widowers over the age of sixty-five in the United States today believe that their deceased husband or wife spends time with them and actually talks to them? Are these people senile? Are they practicing wish fulfillment? Do the answers to these questions really matter?

No.

I wish when my mother died twenty-five years ago that someone had told me it didn't take a fancy ritual, a trip to the local psychic, or delving into things I might have been afraid of to talk to my mother. Modern religion, by accident or design, has not equipped us to handle the personal grieving process, and has frightened us into often doing nothing at all. You arrange and attend the funeral, you light a candle, everyone pats you on the back and hands you a box of tissues—and you're stuck with your thoughts, your fears, and your pain.

In this chapter I've provided you with several techniques to attempt to help you in handling death. Some of these practices are simple, where others are more complicated. If something doesn't feel right to you in any of these techniques, either change them to suit your needs or don't do them at all. There is no religious bias here—just you and me—and again, there is nothing frightening, strange, or sinful in talking to, or honoring, a deceased loved one.

They Can Hear You

Many people say, "I'm not talking to my mother (or father). They can't hear me anyway because they're in heaven (or wherever)"—which enforces our feeling of alienation when confronting death.

Well.

The dead *can* hear you. They *will* listen, and they *will* help you when you need them, if they can. What proof do I have? The hundreds of people I've talked to all over the United States. These aren't the rich, the famous, or the popular. These are people just like you and me. They work in grocery stores, the corporate office, the garage, even nuclear power plants—and they all tell me stories of talking to loved ones who have passed over to the Other Side, and how their lives changed because they had done so. These people aren't out to impress anyone, make money from their stories, or even find themselves in the limelight. The ancient Celts knew that interaction with dead loved ones would not hurt them, nor would their lives be impacted in a negative way, which is how Samhain came about in the first place. Perhaps, over the ravages of time, we've lost some of that spiritual innocence that assisted the Celts when they welcomed the dead into their homes on Samhain, treating the holiday as a happy affair rather than a dark, morose one.

What often stops us from speaking to the dead?

Our fear.

And, perhaps, our guilt.

What I Didn't Get to Tell You

I think the hardest thing for us to deal with when a loved one has passed away, especially if the parting has been sudden, is that we didn't get to say good-bye or to explain something that was important in our relationship. Our current culture does not allow us to speak to the dead. People make fun of us and tell us we are nuts, superstitious, or even sinful, which keeps us from exercising our natural desire to speak to loved ones who have passed beyond the veil. The holiday of Samhain, in its simplistic, pagan beauty, reminds us that our ancient ancestors felt the same needs and desires that we do.

When a loved one dies, the most significant slice in our lives comes from the perceived severing of communication—something humans (even the most private ones) cannot seem to do without. You can't call that person on the phone, hop in your car and drive over to see them, get on the computer and send them e-mail or catch them in a chat room, or walk into the kitchen and say something. You may feel guilty that you didn't say you were sorry for a minor infraction or a situation that remained between you, creating a chasm in your relationship that you thought you'd deal with sometime. And now—there's no time. Feelings of guilt and loneliness deepen the grief process, and we try to shove the whole mess away to a far little corner of our minds, locked in a little mental box that we dare not touch.

Our very first step in dealing with death should be the assurance from our religious leaders, our peers, and our family that we certainly can communicate with the dead. It truly is okay to talk "to the air." You *need* to do it. The deceased needs to hear you, too. Go ahead and tell them what's on your mind—that you miss them, even that you are angry with them for leaving you. That's okay too.

Do you have to light candles and go to a dark, spooky place at midnight? Do you have to conduct a séance? Use a Ouija board? Absolutely not. You can sit in the broad daylight under a tree, if you like, to carry on your conversation. You can talk to them in the laundry room while you're doing your wash, or in the garage while you're fixing your car.

I carried a lot of grief over things left undone with my mother, and I carried that emotional garbage for over twenty years. As soon as I began talking to her, many things changed for the better for me. Don't wait like I did.

A Simple Ritual to Receive Answers from the Dead

For this section I contacted a reliable individual who is well known for working with police from different areas of the country to find missing persons, and who does private readings for individuals who wish to connect with deceased loved ones.

> Salt
> 1 purple candle
> Incense (your choice or use Morgana's blend, page 133)
> Bell
> An object that belonged to the deceased or their picture
> Their favorite flower as a gift of honor, optional

Choose whom you wish to speak to, such as your mother, sibling, good friend, father, grandparents, and so on. I don't advise contacting anyone you didn't know personally, nor do I advocate contacting someone who had a personality disorder. Sprinkle the salt in a circle around you, or sprinkle a salt circle around the base of the purple candle. Light the candle. Light the incense. Carry the incense to the four quarters, beginning with the north, then to the east, to the south, and to the west, asking for protection and blessings. Put the incense beside the candle. You have just created sacred space. Ring the bell three times.

Sit quietly and talk to your deceased loved one. You may feel a slight movement of air, the lights might flicker, et cetera, but most often you will hear your loved one in your mind. In the majority of cases they will sound as they did in life, including speech patterns, favorite sayings, and so on. There is nothing to be afraid of. Just remember the dead weren't perfect when they were living, therefore they are not unutterably correct in death either. If they loved you, they will do the best they can for you, but don't pattern your life entirely on the information you receive.

If your loved one has died recently, they may not be able to communicate with you immediately. There appears to be an acclimation period after death that is different for each individual, and they must learn how to communicate with you. If you don't receive any information this time around, try again at a different time. The reincarnation schedule is also different for each individual. A few will be reborn almost immediately, where others may wait two hundred years. Some experts feel the general earth-time span between lives averages from fifty to seventy-five years.[1]

When you have finished speaking to the loved one, burn additional incense as a gift of honor, say good-bye, and extinguish the candle.

Ancestral Altars

Researching the Celts, Samhain, and the Mexican and South American customs of the Day of the Dead, we learned that altars designed for the dead are not uncommon, nor are they in any way evil or unsavory. Here, the altar becomes a focal point of honor and a physical connection from yourself to a specific person you loved who has died, or the altar can encompass your lineage of ancestors. Many magickal people and individuals of various religions keep such an altar in their homes all year round. If this makes you uncomfortable, then consider making such an altar only through the month of October, or the last week of the harvest month in your area. If you live below the equator, then your seasons will be different than those experienced by individuals in America or Europe.

Why would we make such an altar? Recognition. Realizing that our spirit lives on after death, and using a physical object or objects to affirm this belief. Understanding that death does not kill the vital essence of who and what we are. Honor. That we continue to give our loving energy to someone we cared about.

What does an altar to the deceased look like? Is there a wrong way to construct such a thing? The altar should look the way you want it to—a pleasing sight. It should not contain anything that you would find offensive or frightening. There is no wrong way to honor the dead, unless you, in some way, pervert their memory. The altar itself can consist of a simple shelf, a small table, the top of your bureau in your room, a flat stone—the surface of the altar does not matter. My ancestral altar is a flat stone on my vanity in my bedroom. I have chosen stone because it is fire safe and belongs to the element of earth. This altar changes as my life changes. I have two significant pictures there—one of my mother when she was sixteen years old, and one of my grandmother holding me when I was three. Although some magickal people would shudder, as the altar is a sacred place meant only for religious purposes, several members of my family use this altar almost every day, as it sits under a large mirror. My teenage girls often set their makeup there, hook up their curling irons and blow dryers, twirl in their outfits, and so on. My husband and sons comb their hair, check their teeth, and do whatever else fellas do in front of a mirror.

What's my point? Remembering those who have died is not a scary thing in our house simply because the altar has become a part of our daily routine. Everyone knows what it is. They know why the pictures are there. They all know I talk to my mother and my grandmother. No one is bothered by it. In fact, my daughters, on occasion, have talked to them, too. Nothing bad happened, and they felt much better afterward.

Offerings to the Dead

Incense, fruit, nuts, harvest items, milk, chocolate, ale, strings of beads, candles, cakes, colorful stones, shells, rose petals, rum, strips of colored paper with words of love or blessings—all of these items have found their way to the altars of the dead all over the world. It is believed that these items carry an energy of their own and that, by offering them to the dead, you are giving the essence of the thing—a quantity of positive energy to deceased. By lighting a candle, you are making a connection from yourself, through the elements of earth, air, and fire, to the Other Side—giving energy and the light of love to someone who has passed over.

Many cultures practice prayers for the dead. These prayers feed our loved ones positive energy so that they may work off any negative karma. Many individuals believe that when the dead reach out from the Other Side to assist you with a problem, or watch over you for your protection, the deceased fulfills a very real function in what makes the world go 'round. These two beliefs take the fear out of death and fill a very real need in the human psyche.

Prayer of Offering

One of the most poignant and powerful things you can ever do (in my mind) is offer a prayer for the dead. This can be done at any time during the year, but we place it here in relation to the significance of Halloween.

1 white votive candle
Offering of your choice
Picture of your loved one

Light a white votive candle. Lay your offering on your ancestral altar, or next to a picture of your special loved one. Hold your hands together in the prayer position. (**Note:** The prayer position that most of us are familiar with actually has magickal significance. When you hold your hands together, palm to palm, you are creating a flow of circular energy from the right palm, up your left arm, through your heart chakra, and down your right arm into your right palm.) Say:

From the dawn of your birth
To the sunset of your death
I honor you.
From the missions you completed
To your duties left undone
I honor you.
From the seasons of your being
Through the cycle of your life
I honor you.
From your time beyond the veil
'Til your earth entrance back again
May the angels support you
May Spirit surround you
May my healing love reach you
From this moment until the end of time.
So mote it be.

Seven-Day Samhain Vigil

This vigil is done in honor of any family member or friend, and is especially thoughtful if that individual passed away in the current year. The practice helps you to reach out and touch the love you once knew and give honor to what that person gave to you in life.

7   candles, style and color of your choice
    Picture of your loved one(s)
7   sticks of incense
    Offering of your choice (roses, beads, and so on)

On October 25 (at the time of your choice), light the first candle. You can say a poem, speak aloud to the deceased, sing a song, or read a passage from a book. Light the incense, and say:

In your honor.

Allow the candle to burn completely. On the following five days, do the same activity with a fresh candle and incense. On October 31, light the candle and the incense and leave an offering such as rose petals, a string of beads, and so on. On November 2, dispose of the candle ends and offering by burying them on your property.

The Dumb Supper

Samhain speaks to us of strong emotions; death, resurrection, of deeply cloaked energies, of shining hope for the future. It is a New Years celebration; our will to face the specter of death without tremor and our desire to know those things that others fear to see.

One of the most inspiring rituals performed at Samhain rises from the enactment of the Silent or Dumb Supper. Along with places set for human guests, the table also holds places for those who have passed beyond the veil. The chair at the head of the table, shrouded in black (or white, as you desire) signifies the place of deity.

Five rules exist for the Dumb Supper:

1. The Dumb Supper should take place in an area that you have made sacred by prayer or other means.

2. All plates, napkins, glasses, and the tablecloth should be black.
3. No one may speak from the moment they enter the feast room. Each person participating should leave the room in silence after the ritual.
4. The feast takes place in candlelight or lamplight.
5. Each living guest should bring a prayer, written on a three-by-five-inch card or small piece of paper, for their ancestors or loved ones. Each living guest can also bring a divination tool of their choice.

The timing of the feast depends on your discretion. Some individuals choose midnight of October 30, October 31, November 4, or November 7. All of these dates coincide with various traditional observances. The number of guests also depends on your choices. You may wish to enact the Silent Supper with family members only, or a group of close friends. This feast works well as a pot luck, where each guest brings a cooked dish of their choice, or you can provide a menu and allow guests to choose what they would like to bring.

Before the supper begins, put a black votive candle on the plate at each empty place, and a white votive candle on the plate at the head of the table. The head of the table represents Spirit or deity. Place your hands on the shrouded chair and invite Spirit into the area. Walk to each place set aside for your ancestors, touch the chair, and explain that this ritual will be done in their honor. The host or hostess of the feast sits in the chair opposite Spirit.

As each person enters the room, they should touch the chair of Spirit, then walk to the ancestral places, putting their prayers under the plate. They may wish to stop and contemplate at a particular chair, say a prayer in their minds, or simply send loving energy.

After everyone has taken a place, all living guests should join hands and pray silently for the blessing of the meal and those present, both living and dead. The host and hostess serve the empty plates, beginning at the head of the table. Continue to serve the living guests in order of age, from oldest to youngest.

Because verbal communication doesn't exist during the feast, the host or hostess carries the responsibility of the needs of the living. You may wish to arrange items normally passed throughout a meal (bread, butter, salt, pepper, condiments, and so on) at both ends of the table to lessen any difficulties experienced by the diners. During the meal, the host or hostess should quietly observe the others present to ascertain anything they might need, such as an extra napkin for a slight spill or the refill of a drink.

At the end of the feast, those at the table again join hands, silently asking for the blessings of Spirit on the living and the dead. On the lead from the host or hostess, the diners leave the feast area. They may wish to stop at the empty places or at the ancestral altar before they leave.

After the diners leave the room, the host or hostess thanks Spirit. The guests may now re-enter the room and help to clean up, perhaps sharing their impressions or any messages they have received during the feast. After dessert has been served and you have cleared the table, it's time to break out the divination tools. Guests can separate by pairs, or you can perform a group divination. Allow the candles to burn until the last guest has gone home, then snuff each candle. Dispose of the candle ends in a living body of water or bury them off your property.

Although you may think that the Dumb Supper will only work for a group of people, this is not the case. A solitary Dumb Supper carries as much impact, if not more, when performed with love in your heart.

The Dumb Supper creates a deeply moving ceremony, teaches group interaction without speech, and allows you to honor those who have passed from this realm to the next as well as acknowledge that Spirit moves with us always, from birth through death.

In Vicksburg, Mississippi, an African-American version of the European Dumb Supper was recorded as follows:

> Two people should cook it together, neither saying a word during the process. Get some dirt from the dead person's grave and set it in a saucer in the middle of the table. Cook something such as turnip greens, that the dead person liked to eat, set the table for three and put up three chairs. Then bless the food without speaking to one another and start in silently to eat. Watch the third plate: Unseen hands will manipulate the fork and knife, greens will be taken from the dish all the time, but the chair will remain vacant. All will be well, but should you speak while your invisible guest is with you the wind will blow, the dogs bark, the chickens cackle and thunder and lightning appears to frighten you.[2]

The Samhain Fire

Although many of us may have homes and a yard, we can't always have a bonfire on our property. If you have a fireplace in your home or apartment, you can substitute that as your need-fire, or you can take an old grill and set it outside and fill with charcoal. Before October 31, collect one 4 to 6-inch stick of birch (for new beginnings), holly (to inspire visions), oak (for strength, healing, and wisdom), pine (prosperity and growth), and a small branch of a different tree of your choice to symbolize something special to you or a goal you wish to manifest. Although you can do this ritual alone, you will also enjoy doing this ritual with family and friends. You don't need to make a big "religious" deal about this ritual if you don't want to.

1   fireplace or grill
1   4 to 6-inch stick birch, holly, oak, pine, and other tree
      of your choice, as explained above
1   thimble per person, half filled with rum, vodka, or
      denatured alcohol (do not give to children)
      Musical instruments or taped music, optional

Urge friends and relatives to bring musical instruments. If no one seems to have the musical gift, then you can truck the boom box outside along with a few of your favorite tapes and CDs.

Begin the ritual by blessing the cold fireplace or grill. Light the fire, and say the following:

By the fire within my heart
I call you forth, O Sacred Flame
Within, without, you both are one
From first creation's light you came.

Ancient sister of the stars,
Daughter of the moon and sun
Come forth in mystic golden light
I greet the south from whence you come.

Arise bright fire into the world!

Arise bright fire into the night!

Arise bright fire by Spirit's hand

Arise bright fire of magick's light.

From the core of earth's bright center

Through the cosmos vast expanses

I call thee forth, O Cleansing Fire

I call thee forth to lift and raise us.

And by the power of the Three

I call the wind and rain and earth

Bring the Light that casts no shadow

And give this Sacred Fire its birth.

—© 1998 David O. Norris,
"Invocation of the Sacred Fire"

Ask Spirit (or the deity of your choice) to enter the area and bring the light of love and joy into your present life and into the future. Once the fire is going well, add the sticks you collected, one at a time, calling out the energies you are invoking. For example: "Pine! I invoke prosperity and abundance."

At this point you can sing songs, recite poetry, or play musical instruments. When the fire starts to die, it is time to honor the dead. In a group, each person steps forward and says a person's name who has passed away, and what they admired about them or what they most remembered about them. Then they throw the contents of their thimble into the fire, speaking the dead person's name loudly and saying, "I honor you!" (Be sure to stand far enough away not to get burned.)

Next, say a prayer that you have written for the occasion. Apples can be thrown into a large fire for the dead. For smaller fires, throw chestnuts. Store-bought pumpkin spice thrown on the fire will create a rainbow of colors and can be used in fire divination. Feasting and merriment then follow this ritual.

Soul Lights

You can make soul lights to set at the quarters of your circle, on your altar to remember loved ones, or on your porch to welcome trick-or-treaters. They are simple to make and a great project for the kids to enjoy.

1 tin can, 15-ounce size or larger, for each family member
   who has passed away
   Nail polish remover
   An old towel
   Hammer and nail
   A design for each can
   Hanging wire
½ cup kitty litter for each can
1 tea candle for each can

Remove the lid from the can and peel off the paper label. Use nail polish remover to clean the can of any remaining glue from the label.

Fill the can with water and freeze.

Place the can on its side on a towel. Punch holes with a hammer and nail in the decorative design you have chosen. Carefully punch the initials of the deceased somewhere on the can. (The frozen water keeps the can from getting dented.) Be sure to punch two holes on either side of the can, ¼-inch from the top, for the wire hanger.

Set the can in a sink or outside until the ice melts.

Dry the can. Loop a length of wire through the two holes and secure by twisting.

When you are ready to use the soul light, pour kitty litter in the bottom. Shake lightly from side to side to even out. Place metal tea candle base securely in kitty litter.

Hang can or set in a safe place while candle is burning.

A Gift for the Dead

Let's face it—wreaths get boring and everybody associates the plastic wreath with grave decorations. You can make this colorful project to take to the cemetery to honor someone who has passed away, or you can put the arrangement on your ancestral altar at home. Of course, if you're not into that, you can always make this project as a centerpiece for your Halloween party, too.

Cardboard tubes from paper towels or toilet paper

Halloween wrapping paper (or black and orange construction paper)

Black and orange glitter

Shoebox lid

Scissors and glue

Dried flowers of assorted lengths

Plastic ghosts, Witches, cats, or whatever suits your fancy

Glue Halloween wrapping paper or construction paper around tubes. Add glitter if you like. Cut off any extra wrapping paper.

Glue Halloween wrapping paper or construction paper around the shoebox lid and cut off any extra.

Write the deceased person's name on a card and place it somewhere on one of the tubes or the shoe box.

Arrange dried flowers and herbs inside each of the tubes. Add the plastic cats, Witches, ghosts, and so on.

Spirit Rattles and Spirit Bowls

Spirit rattles are made from dried gourds and used to call forth the spirits of the ancestors in hopes of bringing their wisdom to the ritual, rite, or bonfire celebration. Gourds fall under the element of water and the influence of the moon, with their main function centering around protection, wisdom, and the calling capability once the rattle has been fashioned by magickal hands and enchanted for that purpose. European folklore indicates that gourds can be hung by the front door during the harvest season to ward against negativity and fascinations. Pieces of gourds carried in the pocket are also said to scare away bad influences.

Gourds take a long time to dry and have a tendency to rot if you don't pay attention to them. If you plan to make a spirit rattle from dried gourds, plan a year ahead. During harvest, pick your favorite gourds and place them in a dry, open, airy space. Turn the gourds often over the succeeding months.

> Gourds
> Dried beans, optional
> Paint, optional
> Strips of colored leather, optional

There are three ways to complete your rattle.

One: Shake rattle after it has dried. If the seeds make a pleasing sound to your ear, you will not need to cut open the rattle. Paint the rattle. Add rawhide and feathers to the handle. Or,

Two: After the gourds have dried, use a thin saw blade to cut off the very top. Hold a handful of dried beans in your hand and enchant them to whisper a calling message to your ancestors and the Great Spirit. If this bothers you, you can always make an angel gourd instead, to call the angels. Put the beans in the gourd. Glue the top back on the gourd. Paint the gourd in vibrant colors or a pattern that is pleasing to you. Some individuals wrap the handle of the gourd with strips of colored leather. Or,

Three: With heavy string and beads, create a netting to surround the ball section of the gourd. Tie securely. This will allow you to enhance the sound without cutting the gourd open.

Design a small ritual to bless your gourd, using holy water and sacred oil. This is called "birthing" the rattle. Use the gourd to call the spirits of the dead on Samhain by shaking the gourd softly and humming or chanting:

> *Spirits north, spirits east*
>
> *Spirits south, spirits west*
>
> *Spirits of the center.*
>
> *Ancestors—I call you*
>
> *Ancestors—I call you*
>
> *Bring me your wisdom.*

Be sure to thank your ancestors when you have finished your ritual or divination session.

Spirit bowls are also made from dried gourds. Allow the gourd to dry, then remove the top and smooth out the inside of the bowl with light grade sandpaper. Paint the outside of the bowl with a design of your choosing. On Samhain, the bowl is filled with holy water and used for scrying.

The Cauldron Wake

Most Americans, unless they come from a strong, ethnic background where funeral customs are held closely to family traditions, do not have an intimate procedure for dealing with death, and often family desires override what close friends (or even the deceased) may have wanted in funeral arrangements. The grief cycle, then, especially for close friends, cannot play out in a natural way. This particular ritual can be used on Halloween, or can be done at an appropriate time after a close friend has passed away.

A cauldron, filled with the deceased's favorite nonalcoholic drink

13 tea candles

Each guest should bring:

Pictures or other items representing the deceased

A snack

A good joke

A memory and lesson the deceased taught them written
on a three-by-five-inch card

Place the cauldron in the center of a table. Put the tea candles around the cauldron on a fire-safe tray. Pictures or other items of the deceased can also go on the table. Each person is to bring a snack, a good joke, and a three-by-five-inch card on which they have written a pleasant memory of an interaction with the deceased and one thing that the deceased taught them. If many people will be attending the wake, then they should be advised beforehand that their "memory" has to be written in five sentences or less.

When all the people have gathered, light the tea candles and turn out the lights in the room. The host or hostess should begin by saying something about why the group has gathered. Then someone steps forward and tells their memory, as well as what the deceased taught them. They then take a clean, disposable cup and dip it in the cauldron, hold up in the air, and say:

I drink to my brother (or sister)
May you find peace and love
On your journey beyond the veil.

The group then responds with the words "Here, here," "So mote it be," "So be it," and so on. That person sits down and the next person does the same thing.

When everyone has finished, the host or hostess brings out the food and someone begins telling their joke, and so on. Laughter releases pain and grief, and many times the jokes will deteriorate into funny stories about the deceased. When the conversation begins to turn to other subjects, the host or hostess should rise and call for one minute of silence for the deceased, which can include a prayer or poem. Then he or she turns on the overhead lights and the party can continue.

I should add one little note here about this particular ritual—the deceased will be there, and they will hear you. If you speak as if the person is in the room, a special energy passes over the group and the time you spend together becomes very intimate, heartwarming, and joyful.

Solitary Samhain Ritual

For those of you who would like to practice the Wiccan way (or already do so), I've included this Samhain ritual for your enjoyment.

3   candles, any color or shape
1   bowl of water
     List of those things you are thankful for, including the rewards
     and blessings you have received this year

For the circle casting, stand in the center of the circle, and say:

I cast the Samhain hedge between the worlds

Be thou the halo of the Goddess

And a protection against all negativity.

Positive energy flows in the name of the God

I hallow this place of Spirit.

For the invocation of deity, sit quietly and hum to yourself, making up your own little melody. Envision a hedge around you, growing and flowering on this autumn eve. Then stand in the center of the room, and say:

Wise Goddess, veiled Huntress, grant me your power.

Wise God, Father of magick and the Wild Host,

Waken your wisdom within me.

By the Hidden Mother and the Hooded Lord,

Ancestral fire I kindle

Spiritual love I invoke.

(Insert your statement of purpose.)

I come from the Void, and to Her, I shall return.

Ancient wisdom is my teacher

Fill me with your velvet truth

Grant me your special power.

I know that there is great comfort in eternal sleep and the dark hours of death.

Tonight I journey there, to meet the ones I love

To find wisdom from the ancients

And to rebirth myself again.

(Light two white candles.)

Read:

Samhain is the celebration of the final harvest—the cycle of life and death.

I am joyful in the rewards I have cultivated this year.

(List your rewards and blessings.)

I stand at the crossroads of yet another year. I welcome purification and renewal.

(Pour water over your hands and allow all negativity to leave your body.)

I honor the dark, as the days get shorter and the nights get longer,

and pledge to use this time for introspection and planning for the future.

At Samhain, I know that the veils are the thinnest between the worlds,

and bid my ancestors to visit tonight at my fires and imbue their wisdom to me.

Light a third candle to signify the dead. For the Samhain Invocation for a Loved One, hold both hands out, palms up. Say:

By the threads that still connect us

By the silver cord unbroken

By the love that is eternal

Now (person's name or "my family"), *I will call you*

As the Western Gate stands open

To that land of golden sunsets.

In that peace that is unending

In that life that is eternal.

On this night of ancient wonder
Where our souls can join together
I'll close my eyes and see you smiling
As I slowly reach to touch you
In that land beyond the dawning
Where your journey never ended
Where the pathway still leads upward
On that circle laid through time.

May the moonlight guide your footsteps
may the starlight be your pathway
As we journey to the center
On this ancient night together
When our souls can be united
When our worlds are now the closest
When the silence choirs our love
When the circle is unbroken.

By the mystery all surrounding
With this breath by which I call you
In the flickering of the firelight
I say your name(s) within my heart
It echoes down through time unending
In the protection of this evening
May your presence wash through me
And together we are one.
You who have passed to another plane
(list friends, relatives, loved ones)
I remember you.

Spend some time meditating, singing, or drumming. When you feel fulfilled, it is time to end the ritual. When you have finished, stand in the middle of the room, and say the following "Benediction" by David O. Norris:

It is time to bid farewell

As this Samhain passes from us

Soon the dawning will embrace us

and the sunset portal close.

Until the turning of the year

We must part for just a while

Yet I know there is no ending

And the silver thread spins outward

To that place where you are going

Until I travel there to meet you

Or your return upon the autumn,

On this sacred night of Spirits

When we shall meet again.

Blessed be.

(Closure)

Great Ancestors,

I thank you for joining me this night.

Relatives and loved ones,

I honor you and wish you sleep well.

May you go in peace.

Great Spirit

Stay with me.

Protect and guide me upon this new year.

So mote it be.

Close your eyes and imagine the circle slowly dissipating. Open your eyes and allow the candles to burn until they are finished. Bury off your property.

The Crossing Ritual

I designed this celebration several years ago to meet the needs of those who have gone through the funeral process and still feel that there are issues left unfinished with a deceased loved one. The crossing ritual is usually done at least one month (or more) after the death, and can be performed in a solitary manner or with a group of friends. Many structured religions fail to acknowledge alternative religions, and therefore general funerary rights do not include any type of structure to meet the needs of those who have practiced an alternative faith. The crossing ritual can assist in filling this gap. I have conducted this rite for individuals of many different standard and alternative religions, to help the living deal with the passing of a loved one. I've written this ritual as though you were conducting the celebration for another person, but you can just as easily perform the same functions for yourself.

You can use this ritual for your Samhain celebration, or any other time throughout the year when you feel the need, either for yourself or for a friend or family member.

A room where you will not be disturbed
A blanket
Soft music
Incense
Purple candle
Salt
A large bowl of water
A clean hand towel
The deceased's favorite flowers
A box of tissues

When your friend arrives, have them sit in the middle of the floor on the blanket. Turn on the soft music. Light the incense and take it to the north, the east, the south, and the west, asking for protection and blessings. Light the purple candle and repeat the same pattern. Sprinkle salt in a circle around your friend. If you have invited other people to attend, have them stand around your friend in a circle formation. They may begin singing, chanting, or playing drums softly.

Have your friend hold their hands over the bowl of water. Begin to gently scoop the water with your hands from the bowl over your friend's hands. Say:

> *I am washing the grief and unhappiness away from your Spirit.*
> *As the water cleanses your hands, it cleanses your whole being.*

Your friend may start to cry at this time. That's okay. Dry their hands carefully with the towel.

Check the music. If the tape is ready to run out, switch sides. Then turn to your friend and ask if they are ready. Walk to the west quarter. Say:

> *Great Gubba, guardian of the Gates of Death,*
>
> *I* (say your name) *request that you open the gates*
>
> *so that only* (say the deceased person's name) *may*
>
> *enter in to this circle so that* (say your friend's name)
>
> *may commune with their loved one.*

Stand sideways to allow the deceased person to pass by you. You might feel a movement of air, smell a sweet odor, or hear footsteps.

Guests should turn their backs to the center of the circle to allow your friend privacy. You can say "All will turn," to give them their cue. Then say:

> **(Friend's name),** *let me know when you are finished by saying "I am ready."*

Turn your back as well. You must all wait patiently until your friend has finished. Again, rather than having taped music, you may all chant very quietly, sing, or drum.

Turn to the west quarter, and say:

> *Great Gubba, it is time for the loved one to depart.*

Step aside and allow the deceased to leave the circle. Take the incense around again, this time beginning at the west, then to the south, then the east, and finally, to the north. Say, "The rite has concluded," and put out the candle.

Give the candle and the flowers to your friend. Tell them they can light the candle any time they wish to talk to their deceased loved one. They may take the flowers to the gravesite, or they may keep them in their home. If you have had guests, this ritual usually finishes with feasting that includes hot as well as cold foods.

Official Funeral of the Black Forest Clan

The following service can be performed with or without the body present; however, we have written the ceremony as if it is being taken place in the funeral home. Lady Jane Phaedra spent months checking with funeral homes and various morticians across the country to determine if they had an objection to Pagan funerals. All those interviewed indicated that they did not discriminate on issues of faith, and would welcome the following service. This service was written by Lady Jane Phaedra.

Deceased's measure—If you can't find it, take another one

Pow-Wow altar set-up—Place the deceased's piece of hearthstone here and use it

Holy water

White sage smudge stick

Incense: Ocean breeze, orchid, sandalwood, jasmine (your choice)

Oils for anointing guests: A mixture of ylang-ylang, rosemary, jasmine, and frankincense

A branch of yew, if available, or dried yew from someone in the Clan

Stones for placing around the container or coffin: Amethyst, bloodstone, chalcedony, copper, geodes, hematite, holed stones, lava, moonstone, obsidian, rhodocrosite, silver, tourmaline

Flowers can be used in place of the stones (or in combination): Crocus, heather, jasmine, lily, lily of the valley (poisonous, not required), lotus, morning glory, water lily (poisonous, not required), ylang-ylang[3]
Note: Use gloves and wash hands immediately after handling poisonous flowers or herbs. Do not touch anything until hands have been washed, especially yourself.

An agenda, which should have the deceased's name, their accomplishments, job, and brief background of their faith. Also, explanation of the rites to be performed and the materials and what they mean. Also, tell the people what to do when, and the words to the music if words are to be sung.

> A picture of the deceased to be placed at the west quarter
> Drums and music makers. (You may want to include all guests
>   in the music with rattles and such, or they may bring their own.)
>   Don't worry, most funeral homes will not mind, but you do need
>   to warn them in advance.

The Preparation. The following people should be at the funeral home at least an hour before the guests arrive (to ensure things progress in a timely manner): The Wiccan High Priestess/High Priest (hereafter HPS/HP) and the Quarters. The HPS/HP is to set up the altar. The HPS/HP prepares the holy water and energy/cleansing poem before anyone else enters. Then they admit those doing the quarter calls and anoint them as they enter the space now cleansed and readied for the circle. Other guests are to remain outside until the set-up has been accomplished.

The HPS or HP does the altar devotion, circle casting, and has had the people chosen to do the quarter calls.

The Pre-Ceremony. The HPS or HP presiding over the funeral will have a supply of holy water with them at all times. This holy water is to be sprinkled on the vessel containing the body or ashes, and is to be sprinkled about the area when and where the services are to be performed. This is to cleanse the area of all negativity that may be lurking around to inhibit the deceased's spirit from doing what is needed to pass over. It will also ensure that the people present will be protected from those negative energies. If desirable, the person presiding may have soft drumming commence at this time. Quarters take up their positions. Drummer sits in the west.

The HPS/HP gathers personal power to be prepared for the ceremony at hand.

The Ceremony. Step One: Cast the circle. (Circle casting written by David O. Norris.)

> *I conjure thee, by Spirit's power,*
> *a Circle now around us stand!*
> *I trace the path between the worlds,*
> *A boundary line of gods and man.*

Once around I trace the path.

Twice, it turns into a flame.

Three times around, a wall of fire

Within whose realm we will remain.

This ground is sacred, consecrated

By the power of earth and air

We conjure fire to cleanse our hearts

And waters deep to guard us here.

In the name of She who watches,

In the name of He who stands

This Circle bright is bound around us

While Spirit works its mighty plan.

As above, from crown of heaven

Now below, it is revealed,

Magic Circle o' Nature's Fortress

By my words your power is sealed!

Blessed be.

Anoint the individuals at the quarters and drummer.

Step Two: Call the quarters. (Stand at each quarter as you intone the words.)

Power of ancient dreams, ancestors of the mysterious north,

come forth o' guardian of the earth. Stand your watch throughout this rite.

Let the North Star crown your brow. Hear this call of Witch and Priest/ess.

Let my words draw you near. Lock the gate that none may pass,

unless they come in love and trust. Blessed be.

Power of ancient dreams, ancestors of the mighty east,
come forth o' guardian of the air. Stand your watch throughout this rite.
Let your wings of intelligence protection be! Hear this call of Witch and Priest/ess.
Let my words draw you near. Lock the gate that none may pass,
unless they come in love and trust. Blessed be!

Power of ancient dreams, ancestors of the mighty south,
come forth o' guardian of the flame. Stand your watch throughout this rite.
May your fiery breath cleanse our work. Hear this call of Witch and Priest/ess.
Let my words draw you near. Lock the gate that none may pass,
unless they come in love and trust. Blessed be!

Power of ancient dreams, ancestors of the mighty west,
come forth o' guardian of the waters. Stand your watch throughout this rite.
May your sweeping waters flow to bring protection all around us.
Hear this call of Witch and Priest/ess. Let my words draw you near.
Lock the gate that none may pass, unless they come in love and trust. Blessed be.

Step Three: Cut the door with your hands, as if parting a curtain.

Once the circle has been cast and the quarters called, you may allow the mourners to enter in order of importance or closeness to the deceased. Depending upon the length of the service, you may want to place chairs in a circle format. You may want to give each person entering a small gift of a stone or metal to be placed in the casket or around the vessel containing the ashes. These stones or metals are enhanced with aiding the deceased in their journey to the Summerland. They should be blessed by the HPS or HP beforehand. Use the list of stones or flowers given earlier under materials needed. Close the door.

Step Four: Statement of why you are here.

Step Five: HPS/HP walks to the west quarter, holds out their hands, and beckons that Spirit allow the deceased to enter the circle. Favorite poetry can be used.

HPS/HP states:

The deceased has entered the circle.

Coveners sing a song chosen by deceased.

HPS and HP invoke the Lord and Lady through song, actions, or poetry.

Step Six: The HPS/HP is to say a few words about the Summerland and who has gone there, what the individual was like, the person's accomplishments, and so on (a Witch's eulogy of sorts). This is to be written by the HPS/HP.

Step Seven: If you have a small group, each person may stand and say something about the deceased. However, if you have ten or more people, don't go there, or you'll be standing by that casket all darned day. Save this type of recognition for the wake. If a large group will be present, preselect individuals and give them a three-minute time limit.

During stages 6 and 7, the drummer may keep a slow, soft drum beat.

Step Eight: Poem is to be read that was designated by the deceased.

Step Nine: Drumming, softly, then gradually raising to a crescendo, with increase of speed and rhythm for three minutes.

Step Ten: Total silence.

Step Eleven: HPS/HP walks to the west gate as if escorting the deceased and bids them safe journey with a blessing.

Step Twelve: Cut the main door.

Step Thirteen: Coveners exit, stopping at West Gate to say farewell (not at body, because the body no longer holds the deceased).

Step Fourteen: Acknowledge deity presence, close quarters, take down circle.

At the Gravesite. Drummers keep a soft, slow beat as mourners arrive. When all have been assembled and the internment is ready, the HPS/HP says another poem here, and each person present is to throw a handful of dirt onto the coffin and say their final good-byes.

Current Druidic All Hallows Practices

By Lady Janette Copeland, founder and Chief Archdruid, Divine Circle of the Sacred Grove Order of Druids.

When Silver asked me to write this paragraph for inclusion in her book on Halloween on the practices that I, my Order, and family perform at this time of the year, I was very flattered. The ways that I follow and teach are a blend of old world and modern demands. Being a child of the forties and a teen of the fifties, my life as a Druid started off very differently then those of today. In those days we only associated with our families, as it was too dangerous to be 'open.' Also, there were no great festivals of like-minded people who gathered for fellowship. It wasn't until after the Korean War that my family and others of our clan even considered exposing ourselves to outsiders.

I am a fifth-generation American on my European side (maternal) and was raised on a ranch in southeastern Texas. While we often went to England for summer holidays, All Hallows was usually celebrated at home. My family have been farmers and ranchers since they came to this country, and our celebrations reflect the classic influences of European and American folk culture as well as Druid training. At All Hallows, I was taught as a young girl, the world comes to an end, and then starts again. So everything that we did, we did to resolve the past and prepare for the future.

When I was young All Hallows was the most special time of the year. It was an exciting time of the year for me, especially since most of the canning and butchering was done and I was able to listen to the elders teach, tell stories, and work the circle. All my aunts, uncles, and cousins would come from around the county and my grandparents were kept busy for months in preparation. My family have been followers of the Druid path for generations. While we were never 'out of the broom closet,' we were able to worship in our own way, in private.

At All Hallows, we would light bonfires, perform the rituals of the season, and do the divination for the coming year. Our rites were performed so that the main part of the ceremony took place at midnight, since this is the hour of the daily cycle that is both the past and the future. This holiday was marked by a very specific form of purification. It was performed at the time when we lit the bonfire. At that time everyone would ready to burn an item from the past year to symbolize the things we needed to release or put to rest. One way we did this was is to write those things we were releasing on a piece of paper. This paper would then be hung from a dead tree or branch, which would be laid at the heart of the Samhain bonfire or cauldron. Before the paper was hung, the individual will meditate on the words and their desires. Then, when they were ready, they would place the paper on the Talan (sacrificial) tree. When the Samhain bonfire was lit, the tree (branch) would burn, and as it burned it would carry away the dross of the dying year. Through this purification we could go into the new year pure and ready to face the winter months. When cool, the ashes of the Samhain fire were ritually scattered on the land at sunrise of All Hallows Day.

One of my favorite memories of this time of the year was the preparation of the season's offerings. As part of our fall harvesting, the people in my clan always put together seasonal wreaths that were used at autumn equinox and All Hallows—these were our seasonal offerings. The wreaths and seed and nut blocks we created were edible, and they served to show that we accepted the responsibility placed upon us by the gods and goddess of the Light while they slept. We understood that the dark season was very difficult on the people and the animals of earth, so during our harvest we created the offerings to give to the creatures of earth. We did this very ritually, with the understanding that we were responsible for the care of the god's creatures in our area.

The interest in Druidism and the rise of neo-Druid orders has been both a blessing and a curse. The Druid families of the Americas and Europe have, for the most part, drawn away from the Pagan movement. Many feel that there is no respect or honor for the old ways as they have been taught and lived for generations. As a result we have lost a number of wonderful teachers who have been treated poorly by impatient students. One of my mentors once told me, "Druidism is dying here in Europe; it is your responsibility to see it does not die everywhere." I have spent over forty years doing just that here in the United States. While I have not always been successful in my ventures, it certainly has been an interesting ride. At All Hallows, I remember my teachers who have passed on. Their lessons still live, their love still flourishes, and their sacrifices still bear fruit.

Summary

From the ritual fires of our ancestors to the varied and joyful practices of today's American Halloween, the original significance of Samhain has not changed. I hope you have enjoyed this little book, and urge you to use your own creative ideas in the harvest celebration of Halloween.

And may you always enjoy the things that go EEEK in the night!

Silver RavenWolf

Notes

1. Michael Newton, Ph.D, *Journey of Souls,* Llewellyn, 1994.

2. Leonard W. Roberts, *South from Hell-fer-Sartin' Kentucky Mountain Folk Tales*, Appalachian Heritage edition, Council of Southern Mountains, Inc., 1961, page 92.

3. Edain McCoy, *Entering the Summerland: Customs and Rituals of Transition into the Afterlife*, Llewellyn Publications, 1996.

Condemned at the Salem Witch Trials, 1692

Bishop, Briget—Hanged June 10

Bradbury, Mary—Convicted September 6; Escaped

Burroughs, Rev. George—Hanged August 19

Carrier, Martha—Hanged August 19

Cloyce, Sara—Convicted September 6; Reprieved

Cory, Giles—Pressed to death September 19

Cory, Martha—Hanged September 22

Eames, Rebecca—Convicted September 1; Reprieved

Esty, Mary—Hanged September 22

Faulkner, Abigail—Convicted; pleaded pregnancy

Foster, Ann—Died in jail

Good, Sarah—Hanged July 19

Hoar, Dorcas—Convicted September 6; Reprieved

Hobbs, Abigail—Convicted September 6; Reprieved

How, Elizabeth—Hanged July 19

Jacobs, George—Hanged August 19

Lacy, Mary—Convicted September 6; Reprieved

Martin, Susanna—Hanged July 19

Nurse, Rebecca—Hanged July 19

Osborne, Sara—Died in jail

Parker, Alice—Hanged September 22

Parker, Mary—Hanged September 22

Proctor, Elizabeth—Convicted; Pleaded pregnancy

Proctor, John—Hanged August 19

Pudeator, Ann—Hanged September 22

Reed, Wilmot—Hanged September 22

Scott, Margaret—Hanged September 22

Tituba—Held in jail

Wardwell, Samuel—Hanged September 22

Wilds, Sarah—Hanged July 19

Willard, John—Hanged August 19

BIBLIOGRAPHY

Articles on Witchcraft, Magic and Demonology: A Twelve-Volume Anthology of Scholarly Articles, edited with introduction by Brian P. Levack, Garland Publishing, Inc., 1992.

Bannatyne, Lesley Pratt, *Halloween—An American Holiday, An American History,* Pelican, 1998.

Baroja, Julio Caro, *World of Witches,* University of Chicago Press, 1961.

Barrick, Mac E. compilation, *German-American Folklore,* American Folklore Series, August House, 1987.

Best, Joel, and Horiuchi, *"The Razor Blade in the Apple: The Social Construction of Urban Legends,"* Social Problems, Volume 32, No. 5, June 1985, pp. 448-449.

Campanelli, Dan, and Pauline, *Halloween Collectables: A Price Guide*, L-W Book Sales, P. O. Box 69, Gas City, IN 46933, 1995.

Cohn, Norman, *Europe's Inner Demons*, Basic Books, Inc., 1975.

Crow, W. B., *A History of Magic, Witchcraft, and Occultism*, Aquarian Press, 1968.

Dale-Green, Patricia, *Cult of the Cat*, Barre Publishing, 1964.

Eichler, Lillian, *The Customs of Mankind*, Nelson Doubleday, Inc. 1924.

Frazer, James George, Sir, F. R. S., F. B. A, *The Golden Bough*, Macmillan Publishing Co., 1978.

Greenway, John, *Folklore of the Great West*, American West Publishing Co., 1970.

Guiley, Rosemary Ellen, *The Encyclopedia of Witches and Witchcraft*, Facts on File, NY, 1989. Focuses on WitchCraft information, including historical data as well as insights into the Craft in America from 1960 to 1985.

Halloween—Its Origins, Rites and Ceremonies in the Scottish Tradition, Albyn Press, 1970.

Harrington, David, and deTraci Regula, *Whispers of the Moon*, Llewellyn Publications, 1996.

Hazlitt, W. C., *Dictionary of Faiths & Folklore Beliefs, Superstitions and Popular Customs*, First Edition 1905 Reeves and Turner, London; current edition Bracken Books, 1995.

Hroch, Miroslav, and Anna Skybova, *Ecclesia Militans—The Inquisition*, Dorset Press, Germany, 1988.

Jones, Prudence, and Nigel Pennick, *A History of Pagan Europe*, Routledge, 1995.

Lee, Karin, *The Halloween Tarot*, U. S. Games Systems, Inc. , 1996.

L'Estrange, Ewen C., *Witch Hunting and Witch Trials*, Dial Press, 1929.

Lindholm, Lars, *Pilgrims of the Night*, Llewellyn Publications, 1993.

Markale, Jean, *The Celts*, Inner Traditions, 1978.

Matthews, Caitlin and John, *The Encyclopaedia of Celtic Wisdom, The Celtic Shaman's Sourcebook*, Element Books Limited, 1994. Website address: http://www.hallowquest.org.uk

McCoy, Edain, *Entering the Summerland: Customs and Rituals of Transition into the Afterlife,* Llewellyn Publications, 1996.

Murray, Margaret A., *The God of the Witches,* Oxford University Press, 1970. Originally published by Sampson Low, Marston, and Co., Ltd., 1931.

Nichols, Ross, *The Book of Druidry,* Thorsons, an imprint of Harper Collins Publishers, 1990.

Pennick, Nigel, *Celtic Sacred Landscapes,* Thames & Hudson, 1996.

Pickering, David, *Dictionary of Superstitions,* Cassell, 1995.

Potter, Carole, *Knock on Wood and other Superstitions,* Bonanza Books, 1983.

Radford, E. and M. A., *Encyclopedia of Superstitions,* The Philosophical Library, 1949.

Randolph, Vance, *Ozark Magick and Folklore,* Dover Publications, Inc., 1964 (which reflects the 1947 original version).

Robbins, Rossel Hope, *Encyclopedia of Witchcraft and Demonology,* Crown Publishers, 1959.

Rose, Carol, *Spirits, Fairies, Leprechauns, and Goblins—An Encyclopedia,* W. W. Norton & Company, 1996.

Santino, Jack, ed. *Halloween and Other Festivals of Life and Death,* The University of Tennessee Press, 1994.

———, *The Hallowed Eve: Dimensions of Culture in a Calendar Festival in Northern Ireland,* The University Press of Kentucky, 1998.

Smith, John Holland, *The Death of Classical Paganism,* Scribner, 1976.

Starkey, Marion, *The Devil in Massachusetts,* Doubleday/Anchor, 1969.

Swanhild, *Holiday Folklore,* Green Man Press, 1990.

Taleja, Tad, "Trick or Treat—PreTexts and Contexts," in *Halloween and Other Festivals of Life and Death* edited by Jack Santino, University of Tennessee Press, 1994.

Walker, Barbara G., *The Woman's Dictionary of Symbols and Sacred Objects,* Harper and Row, 1988.

———, *The Woman's Encyclopedia of Myths and Secrets,* Harper and Row; 1983.

Walker, Mark, *The Great Halloween Book,* Liberty Publishing Company, 1990.

Waring, Philippa, *A Dictionary of Omens and Superstitions,* Ballantine Books, 1978.

Wilde, Lyn Webster, *Celtic Women in Legend, Myth and History,* Sterling Publishing Company, Inc., 1997.

Index

Note: All recipe, ritual, and spell titles are in bold type.

☾ ORDER LLEWELLYN BOOKS TODAY!

Llewellyn publishes hundreds of books on your favorite subjects! To get these exciting books, including the ones on the following pages, check your local bookstore or order them directly from Llewellyn.

Order Online:

Visit our website at www.llewellyn.com, select your books, and order them on our secure server.

Order by Phone:

- Call toll-free within the U.S. at 1-877-NEW-WRLD (1-877-639-9753). Call toll-free within Canada at 1-866-NEW-WRLD (1-866-639-9753)
- We accept VISA, MasterCard, and American Express

Order by Mail:

Send the full price of your order (MN residents add 7% sales tax) in U.S. funds, plus postage & handling to:

Llewellyn Worldwide
P.O. Box 64383, Dept. 1-56718-719-6
St. Paul, MN 55164-0383, U.S.A.

Postage & Handling:

Standard (U.S., Mexico, & Canada). If your order is:
Up to $25.00, add $3.50
$25.01 - $48.99, add $4.00
$49.00 and over, FREE STANDARD SHIPPING
(Continental U.S. orders ship UPS. AK, HI, PR, & P.O. Boxes ship USPS 1st class. Mex. & Can. ship PMB.)

International Orders:
Surface Mail: For orders of $20.00 or less, add $5 plus $1 per item ordered. For orders of $20.01 and over, add $6 plus $1 per item ordered.

Air Mail:
Books: Postage & Handling is equal to the total retail price of all books in the order.
Non-book items: Add $5 for each item.

Orders are processed within 2 business days. Please allow for normal shipping time.
Postage and handling rates subject to change.

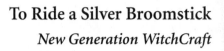

To Ride a Silver Broomstick
New Generation WitchCraft

SILVER RAVENWOLF

Throughout the world there is a new generation of Witches—people practicing or wishing to practice the craft on their own, without an in-the-flesh magickal support group. *To Ride a Silver Broomstick* speaks to those people, presenting them with both the science and religion of WitchCraft, allowing them to become active participants while growing at their own pace. It is ideal for anyone: male or female, young or old, those familiar with WitchCraft, and those totally new to the subject and unsure of how to get started.

Full of the author's warmth, humor, and personal anecdotes, *To Ride a Silver Broomstick* leads you step-by-step through the various lessons with exercises and journal writing assignments. This is the complete WitchCraft 101, teaching you to celebrate the Sabbats, deal with coming out of the broom closet, choose a magickal name, visualize the Goddess and God, meditate, design a sacred space, acquire magickal tools, design and perform rituals, network, spell cast, perform color and candle magick, divination, healing, telepathy, psychometry, astral projection, and much, much more.

ISBN 0-87542-791-X
320 pp., 7 x 10, illus., softcover $14.95

To Stir a Magick Cauldron

A Witch's Guide to Casting and Conjuring

Silver RavenWolf

The sequel to the enormously popular *To Ride a Silver Broomstick: New Generation Witchcraft.* This upbeat and down-to-earth guide to intermediate-level witchery was written for all Witches—solitaries, eclectics, and traditionalists. In her warm, straight-from-the-hip, eminently knowledgeable manner, Silver provides explanations, techniques, exercises, anecdotes, and guidance on traditional and modern aspects of the Craft, both as a science and as a religion.

Find out why you should practice daily devotions and how to create a sacred space. Learn six ways to cast a magick circle. Explore the complete art of spell-casting. Examine the hows and whys of Craft laws, oaths, degrees, lineage, traditions, and more. Explore the ten paths of power, and harness this wisdom for your own spell-craft. This book offers you dozens of techniques—some never before published—to help you uncover the benefits of natural magick and ritual and make them work for you—without spending a dime!

Silver is a "working Witch" who has successfully used each and every technique and spell in this book. By the time you have done the exercises in each chapter, you will be well-trained in the first level of initiate studies. Test your knowledge with the Wicca 101 test provided at the back of the book and become a certified Witch! Learn to live life to its fullest through this positive spiritual path.

ISBN 1-56718-424-3
288 pp., 7 x 10, illus., softcover   **$16.95**

To Light a Sacred Flame
Practical WitchCraft for the Millennium

SILVER RAVENWOLF

Silver RavenWolf continues to unveil the mysteries of the Craft with *To Light a Sacred Flame*, which follows her best-selling *To Ride a Silver Broomstick* and *To Stir a Magick Cauldron* as the third in the "New Generation WitchCraft" series, guides to magickal practices based on the personal experiences and successes of a third-degree working Witch.

Written for today's seeker, this book contains techniques that unite divinity with magick, knowledge, and humor. Not structured for any particular tradition, the lessons present unique and insightful material for the solitary as well as the group. Explore the fascinating realms of your inner power, sacred shrines, magickal formularies, spiritual housecleaning, and the intricacies of ritual. This book reveals new information that includes a complete discussion on the laws of the Craft, glamouries, and shamanic Craft rituals, including a handfasting and wiccaning (saining).

ISBN 1-56718-721-8
320 pp., 7 x 10 $14.95

TO ORDER, CALL 1-877-NEW-WRLD
Prices subject to change without notice

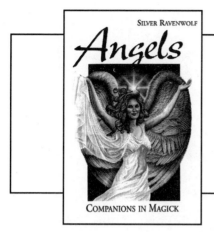

SILVER RAVENWOLF

Angels

COMPANIONS IN MAGICK

Angels
Companions in Magick

SILVER RAVENWOLF

Angels do exist. These powerful forces of the Universe flow through human history, riding the currents of our pain and glory. You can call on these beings of the divine for increased knowledge, love, patience, health, wisdom, happiness and spiritual fulfillment. Always close to those in need, they bring peace and prosperity into our lives.

Here, in this complete text, you will find practical information on how to invite these angelic beings into your life. Build an angelic altar . . . meet the archangels in meditation . . . contact your guardian angel . . . create angel sigils and talismans . . . work magick with the Angelic Rosary . . . talk to the deceased. You will learn to work with angels to gain personal insights and assist in the healing of the planet as well as yourself.

Angels do not belong to any particular religious structure—they are universal and open their arms to humans of all faiths, bringing love and power into people's lives.

ISBN 1–56718–724–2
288 pp., 7 x 10, illus., softcover $14.95

Teen Witch

Wicca for a New Generation

SILVER RAVENWOLF

Teenagers and young adults comprise a growing market for books on WitchCraft and magick, yet there has never been a book written specifically for the teen seeker. Now, Silver RavenWolf, one of the most well-known Wiccans today and the mother of four young Witches, gives teens their own handbook on what it takes and what it means to be a Witch. Humorous and compassionate, *Teen Witch* gives practical advice for dealing with everyday life in a magickal way. From homework and crabby teachers to parents and dating, this book guides teens through the ups and downs of life as they move into adulthood. Spells are provided that address their specific concerns, such as the "Call Me Spell" and "The Exam Spell."

Parents will also find this book informative and useful as a discussion tool with their children. Discover the beliefs of WitchCraft, Wiccan traditions, symbols, holidays, rituals, and more.

ISBN 1-56718-725-0
288 pp., 7 x 10, softcover $12.95

Witches' Night Out

SILVER RAVENWOLF

Now, from the author of *Teen Witch*—the wildly popular guide to Witchcraft—comes the first in a new series of spellbinders written specifically for teens. Featuring the five characters on the cover of Teen Witch, these fictional books will focus on the strength, courage, and willpower of the teens to overcome seemingly insurmountable obstacles, with enough authentic magickal practice thrown in to keep you on the edge of your seat. Every book features a spell that readers can do themselves.

Main character Bethany Salem, 16, is on her own most of the time. Five years ago her mother died, leaving her in the care of her father, a New York City cop, who has deposited her in the suburbs with their Santerian housekeeper.

The adventure begins when enterprising Bethany starts a coven with her friends. In *Witches' Night Out*, the teens find themselves sleuthing to determine who caused the fatal automobile wreck of their friend Joe.

ISBN 1-56718-728-5
240 pp.,4 ⅛ x 6 ¾, softcover   **$4.99**

TO ORDER, CALL 1-877-NEW-WRLD
Prices subject to change without notice

Witches' Key to Terror

SILVER RAVENWOLF

More occult fiction just for teens . . .

From the author of *Teen Witch*—the wildly popular guide to Witchcraft—comes the third installment in the "Witches' Chillers" series of spellbinders. Feisty teens of different races and different backgrounds make up the WNO (Witches' Night Out coven). Can they withstand the pressures of growing up and working magick at the same time? Each book focuses on their strength, courage, and willpower to overcome seemingly insurmountable obstacles, with enough authentic magickal practice thrown in to keep you on the edge of your seat.

In this newest installment, sixteen-year-old Cricket Bindart finds a dead rabbit hanging from her mailbox, with a threatening note attached. Since she is home schooled at her family's orchard and not allowed to associate with public school kids, she calls on the Goddess of the Fields to bring her Witches who can help her find the stalker and save her farm from foreclosure. Enter the WNO coven. Do you dare to join them?

0-7387-0049-5
272 pp.,4 ⅛ x 6 ¾ $4.99

TO ORDER, CALL 1-877-NEW WRLD
Prices subject to change without notice

Solitary Witch

The Ultimate Book of Shadows for the New Generation

SILVER RAVENWOLF

The BIG book for Pagan teens . . .

This book has everything a teen Witch could want and need between two covers: a magickal cookbook, encyclopedia, dictionary, and grimoire. It relates specifically to today's young adults and their concerns, yet is grounded in the magickal work of centuries past.

Information is arranged alphabetically and divided into five distinct categories: (1) Shadows of Religion and Mystery, (2) Shadows of Objects, (3) Shadows of Expertise and Proficiency, (4) Shadows of Magick and Enchantment, and (5) Shadows of Daily Life. It is organized so readers can skip over the parts they already know, or read each section in alphabetical order.

- By the author of the best-selling *Teen Witch* and mother of four teen Witches
- A jam-packed learning and resource guide for serious young Witches
- All categories are discussed in modern terms and their associated historical roots
- A training companion to *Teen Witch* and *To Ride a Silver Broomstick*

0-7387-0319-2

8 x 10, 608 pp., 53 illus., appendices, index $19.95

Samhain Benediction

It is time to bid farewell
As this Samhain passes slowly
Soon the dawning will embrace us
And the sunset portal close
Until the turning of the year
We must part for just a while
Yet I know there is no ending
And the golden thread spins outward
To that place where you are going
Until I travel there to meet you
Or you return upon the autumn
On that sacred night of Spirits
When we shall meet again
Blessed be.

—©1998 DAVID O. NORRIS